1 ST. PETER'S
2 PAULINE CHAPEL
3 BRONZE DOOR
4 ST. PETER'S SQUARE, OR PIAZZA
5 COLONNADE
6 HOLY OFFICE
7 VATICAN WALLS
8 SACRISTY OF ST. PETER'S
9 RESIDENCE OF STAFF
10 RAILROAD STATION
11 MOSAIC STUDIO
12 RADIO STATION
13 ETHIOPIAN COLLEGE
14 WALL BUILT BY POPE LEO IV
15 GOVERNOR'S PALACE
16 VATICAN GARDENS
17 CASINO OF POPE PIUS IV
18 PICTURE GALLERY
19 ENTRANCE TO MUSEUMS
20 MUSEUMS
21 COURT OF THE PINE
22 BRACCIO NUOVO, OR NEW WING
23 COURT OF THE PRINTING HOUSE
24 LIBRARY
25 BELVEDERE COURT
26 POWER PLANT AND HEATING PLANT
27 SISTINE CHAPEL
28 GALLERIES OF RAPHAEL

29 COURT OF ST DAMASUS
30 POPE'S APARTMENTS
31 POST OFFICE AND TELEGRAPH STATION
32 BELVEDERE PALACE
33 GARAGE
34 MACHINE SHOP
35 OFFICE OF OSSERVATORE ROMANO
36 ST ANNA'S, THE PARISH CHURCH OF THE VATICAN
37 GATE OF ST. ANNA
38 BARRACKS OF SWISS GUARDS
39 ANCIENT WALL, LEADING TO THE CASTLE OF ST. ANGELO

VICTOR KEUPING

WHITE SMOKE
OVER THE VATICAN

DON SHARKEY

The Bruce Publishing Company
Milwaukee

Nihil obstat: H. B. Ries, Censor librorum
Imprimatur: ✠ Moyses E. Kiley, Archiepiscopus Milwaukiensis
November 26, 1943

(Fourth Printing — 1947)

TO
MY MOTHER AND FATHER

CONTENTS

LIST OF ILLUSTRATIONS

PART I

Introduction

Chapter I

ACROSS NINETEEN CENTURIES

IN THE beautiful Vatican gardens there stand two tall slender towers of steel. They are easily recognized as supports for the antenna of a broadcasting station. Near by is a square one-story building covered with tiles. These very modern structures stand out in startling contrast with the ancient gardens surrounding them and with the venerable buildings in the other parts of Vatican City.

The tiled building houses some of the most modern broadcasting equipment to be found anywhere on earth. This is station HJV, the Holy Father's own radio station. It was installed under the supervision of the late Guglielmo Marconi, inventor of radio. Six hundred million listeners, one third of the world's population, are estimated to have heard Pope Pius XI in 1931 when he made the first papal broadcast in history. In the course of his address on this occasion he used a quotation from Isaias: "Hear, O ye far islands . . . hear, ye distant peoples."

Over the entrance to the station are the words: "In order that the voice of the Supreme Pastor — by the ether waves — for the glory of Christ and the salvation of souls — may be heard to the ends of the world."

The station is used by the Papal Secretary of State in transmitting orders to his diplomatic representatives abroad. Each representative has been given a ten-tube short-wave set and has been assigned wave lengths and hours of transmission.

The Vatican is always ready to make use of the latest developments of science in order to help the cause of the Church and to spread the word of Christ.

Beneath the high altar of St. Peter's lies a network of low-ceilinged, dimly lighted grottoes or crypts. These crypts are seen by only a very few of the thousands of pilgrims who visit the Vatican each year. They are the remains of an earlier church which once stood on this spot, and they are the burial places of many of the Popes.

In one of these crypts there is a tiny chapel. The visitor who comes upon this chapel falls to his knees in awed reverence; he is in one of the most sacred shrines in all Christendom. This is the Chapel of the Tomb of St. Peter. Under the altar lies the grave of the Prince of the Apostles, the first Supreme Pontiff of Christ's own Church!

St. Peter was put to death in the Garden of Nero, where the Vatican now stands, and was buried there. At one time the body was moved with that of St. Paul to a vault on the Appian Way, but it was later taken back to its original resting place. In A.D. 306, Constantine the Great began the erection of a church over the tomb. This was the first Basilica of St. Peter. Only once in the sixteen centuries that have passed since then has the tomb been seen by mortal eyes.

In 1602 or 1603, workmen laying the foundation for the new church accidentally fractured the ancient vault, revealing its interior. Pope Clement VIII rushed to the scene with Cardinal Bellarmine and several other cardinals. Falling to his knees the Pontiff gazed reverently at the gold cross on the bronze encasement of the sarcophagus. The cross had been placed there by

Helena, the mother of Constantine. The opening was walled up in the presence of Pope Clement VIII and has remained sealed ever since.

St. Peter's tomb and the Vatican radio station! In time, they are separated by nineteen centuries, almost the entire Christian era. But in actual distance they are not very far apart. One is under St. Peter's Basilica; the other is behind it. The first Pope, appointed by our Blessed Lord Himself, was put to death and buried in the Vatican. His modern successor lives and labors there, and when he chooses addresses the faithful throughout the world, sending his voice into their homes. How St. Peter would have welcomed an opportunity of this kind!

St. Peter's tomb and the Vatican radio station! An early and a recent chapter in a story that has been going on for nineteen hundred years and will continue until time itself comes to an end. The story is an engrossing one. It tells of heartaches and defeats and also of glorious triumphs. It is the story of Christianity.

No book could tell the complete story of the Vatican. No great library of books could do it; the subject is too vast. In this book we shall look into some of the outstanding developments in the history of the Vatican, inquire into the government of the Catholic Church, and see Vatican City as it is today, a country unique in the world, a country so small that it is entirely surrounded by a "foreign" city.

The head of this country has no great standing army. He has no navy, no air force. He has no desire for land outside. His own tiny domain, the size of an eighteen-hole golf course, is enough for him. Yet the Pope's influence knows no territorial bounds. The millions of people who look to him for spiritual leadership are spread throughout the entire world.

If, when you have read this book, you know a little more about the Vatican than you do now, the purpose of the author will have been accomplished.

PART II
The Pope

Chapter II

A SHEPHERD LAYS DOWN HIS STAFF

POPE PIUS XI was dying. Several times within the past few months it had seemed that the Pontiff was at the point of death, but each time he had staged a remarkable recovery. This time, however, the doctors held out no hope. The end, they said, was very near.

Pope Pius had lived for eighty-two years, the last seventeen of which he had spent as Supreme Shepherd of the Roman Catholic Church — seventeen years of toil and turmoil during which the Church had made great progress despite the opposition that it had encountered from so many quarters. Even now, while he was still living, Pope Pius XI was acknowledged as one of the great Popes of history. Now he was about to lay down his staff.

It was in the early morning hours of February 10, 1939. Rome was still sleeping. In the Papal apartment the lights of many candles flickered on the serene countenance of the dying Pope and on the sorrowful faces of the Cardinals and the others grouped about him. In the next room the high dignitaries of the official family formed a guard of honor. The Pope's sacristan, Monsignor De Romanis, gave him the Sacrament of Extreme Unction. The generals of the great religious orders gave the

Pontiff the special indulgences which they have the privilege of conferring. The sacristan repeated the moving prayer *Proficiscere anima christiana* (Depart, Christian soul). Clasping a crucifix and with a murmured prayer for peace on his lips, Pope Pius XI drew his last breath. Immediately, a Mass for the repose of his soul was begun in his private chapel a few feet away.

In vestments of deep violet red, the color of mourning, Cardinal Pacelli, the Cardinal Camerlengo, approached the bed. He gazed down at the body of the Pontiff with whom he had been associated for so many years. Then he turned to the grieving prelates.

"The Pope is truly dead," he said.

All fell to their knees and recited the *De Profundis*.

When this prayer was concluded, the Fisherman's Ring was drawn from the Pope's finger and given to Cardinal Pacelli, to be broken at the next meeting of cardinals. At the same time, the matrix with which the papal bulls were sealed was scraped. (These two things signify Papal authority. Their destruction signifies that for the time being there is no such authority.)

The certificate of death was signed by the cardinals and sealed. Next the penitentiaries, or priest-confessors of St. Peter's, entered to dress the body in the Papal robes. Cardinal Pacelli withdrew to notify the diplomatic corps and the Vatican officials. At the door of the Pope's apartment the Swiss guards stood with lowered swords in sign of mourning.

The sad news of the Pope's death was conveyed to the world by the tolling of the "Campanone," the deep-toned master bell of St. Peter's. The bells of Rome's 400 churches were ringing the Angelus when the tolling was heard. Immediately they took up the sad refrain.

The people, hearing the tolling of the bells, breathed a silent prayer for the repose of the soul of the Pontiff. "A great Pope has left us," they said.

That, briefly, is the story of the death of Pope Pius XI. Substitute different names and dates and change a few minor details and it is also the story of the death of a great number of Popes. The ceremonies attending the death, election, and coronation of a Supreme Pontiff have centuries of tradition behind them. The greatest innovation in 1939 was the use of the radio in transmitting the news. People sitting by their loud-speakers in all parts of the world were informed of the Pope's death almost as soon as it took place.

Universal mourning followed the sad news that Pope Pius XI had died. Catholics and non-Catholics, rich and poor, felt that they had lost a kind and good father. Churches were draped in black. Flags were lowered to half-mast. Messages of sympathy from the world's leaders poured into the Vatican. The United States Congress and the French Chamber of Deputies adjourned out of respect for the memory of Pope Pius. Thousands of people all over the world offered prayers for the repose of the Pope's soul and for God's guidance in the choice of a successor.

For a few hours the Pontiff's body was left in the quiet of his room. Then the penitentiaries dressed it in white with a red velvet cape edged in white fur and placed it on a litter or stretcher. A solemn procession consisting of the Palatine guards, the chaplains, the chamberlains, the noble guards, and the cardinals, all bearing torches, escorted the body to the Sistine Chapel. There, on a high, draped platform it rested peacefully with Michelangelo's painting of the Last Judgment as a background. Cardinals, diplomats, Vatican officials, the Crown Prince of Italy, and members of the nobility, came to mourn and pray. It was in this same chapel, almost exactly 17 years before, that the Pope's election had taken place.

The next day, February 11, the day on which he was to have entered St. Peter's joyously to celebrate the tenth anniversary

of the signing of the Lateran Treaty, the body of the Holy
Father was borne into the Basilica by sorrowful attendants to
the accompaniment of the tolling bells. The gold hangings that
had been put up in St. Peter's for the coming celebration of
the anniversaries of the signing of the Lateran Treaty and the
coronation of Pope Pius had been hastily taken down, and black
ones put up instead.

The body was placed on a sloping, red-velvet-draped table in
the Chapel of the Sacrament. Four noble guards stood at each
corner with drawn swords. Vast crowds thronged to St. Peter's
for a last look at their beloved Pontiff. In the crowds were people
of all kinds: wealthy merchants and poor shopkeepers, city
people and peasant farmers, the middle classes, members of
religious orders in robes of all colors — people by the thousands
all came to pay their last respects to the Father of Christendom.

On Sunday, February 12, the seventeenth anniversary of the
coronation of Pope Pius, the first of the nine prescribed funeral
services was held in the canon's choir.

The burial took place on the evening of February 14. About
8000 persons including the diplomatic corps, members of the
Roman nobility, the Swiss guards, the noble guards, the Papal
gendarmes, and specially invited guests were admitted to the
Basilica for the event. This small number of persons seemed
like a mere handful in the vast structure, and the emptiness of
the church added a dismal note to the ceremonies. A choir
chanted solemnly, and when it paused the sad tolling of bells
could be heard. The body of the Pope was laid in three coffins,
one of cypress, one of lead, and one of oak, resting one within
the other. Two veils of white silk were placed over his face and
hands. An elegy was read in Latin recounting the principal acts
of his pontificate. A great clanking echoed and re-echoed
through the vast Basilica as the coffins were closed and sealed.
The triple coffin was covered by a purple pall and carried to the
Confession where the cardinals had now gathered. The

sanpietrini, or Vatican workmen, slowly lowered the coffin into a little wagon and rolled it into the grottoes beneath the Basilica. There Pope Pius XI had had a tomb prepared for himself near the tombs of Pope Pius X who had appointed him librarian, and Pope Benedict XV who had made him a cardinal.

Thus a great Pope left the scene of his earthly labors.

For a while the Church was without a head. The cardinals, who are the highest persons in the Church next to the Pope, became the governing body. Cardinal Pacelli, the Camerlengo, in consultation with the heads of the three cardinal orders, bishops, priests, and deacons, attended to the details of the burial of Pope Pius XI and the coming Papal election. No important decisions regarding the affairs of the Church or State could be made.

The attention of the entire world was now focused upon the Vatican. Cardinals were hurrying to Rome from all over the world to take part in the election of a new Pope. Everyone wondered who would guide the Church through the critical years that lay ahead.

Chapter III

WHITE SMOKE OVER THE VATICAN

IT WAS the spring of 1271. Seventeen cardinals were meeting in the episcopal palace in the town of Viterbo, Italy, for the purpose of electing a Pope. They had been meeting for two years and nine months and seemed just as far from a decision as when they had started.

Such a long delay in the election of a Pope is serious. While the Papal throne is vacant, nothing of importance can be decided. Many persons, including St. Bonaventure, had called the attention of the cardinals to the gravity of the situation and had begged them to arrive at a decision. Still the cardinals failed to agree.

The exasperated citizens of Viterbo decided that something must be done. The city authorities ordered the doors of the palace boarded up. The Savelli, one of the noble families, were made the guardians to see that no one entered or left the palace. (Their descendants, the Chigi, are marshals of the conclave to this day.) It was thought that if the cardinals were kept enclosed until they had arrived at a decision they would agree much more quickly. The cardinals were still unable to agree, but they were anxious to be released from their confinement, so they named a commission of six cardinals and said that the choice of a Pope should be up to them. The commission elected Pope Gregory X.

This was the first time that the cardinals were kept under

lock and key while electing a Pope, and it was the beginning of a custom which has lasted for almost seven centuries. After his election Pope Gregory X determined that such a long delay should not occur again. In 1274 he set forth the rules of the *conclave*. Some changes have been made in these rules, but essentially they are the same today as they were in 1274. For short periods the rules of the conclave were suspended, but each time the Papal election took so long that it was necessary to put them back in force.

Before going any further, it might be well to explain that the word conclave has two meanings. It means the assembly of cardinals which has as its purpose the election of a Pope; it also means the enclosed place in which they meet for this purpose.

Pope Gregory X said that the conclave should begin ten days after the death of a Pope. This rule remained in force for more than seven centuries. At that time most of the cardinals were in Europe and could easily get to Rome within the prescribed time. With the discovery of new lands, however, and the consequent spread of the Church, there were cardinals in such faraway places as the United States, Canada, and Australia. Ten days proved too short a time to allow them to get to Rome. Cardinal Gibbons took part in the election of Pope Pius X, in 1903, but he was able to do so only because he had left Baltimore twelve days before Leo XIII died. Cardinal O'Connell of Boston twice arrived too late to take part in the voting. In 1922 he was just one hour too late. At his request, one of the first acts of Pope Pius XI was to extend the time between the death of the Pope and the beginning of the conclave to fifteen days. It was further stipulated that if all the cardinals were not in Rome by that time another three days could be allowed to them.

In 1939, when Pope Pius XII was elected, three American cardinals took part in the voting for the first time in history:

Cardinals Dougherty of Philadelphia, Mundelein of Chicago, and O'Connell of Boston.

With the increasing speed of steamships and the rapid development of air travel, perhaps it will soon be possible to return to the ten-day rule.

Sixty-two cardinals took part in the conclave that began March 1, 1939, eighteen days after the death of Pope Pius XI. Of the 62, 35 were Italians and 27 were from other countries. Besides the three cardinals from the United States there were one from Canada and two from South America, making six in all from the Western Hemisphere. France had six, Germany four, Spain three, Great Britain one, Poland one, and Ireland one.

Fifty-two of the cardinals had been raised to their rank by Pope Pius XI. During his long reign he had created 76 cardinals. Only six of those taking part in this conclave had been present at the election of Pope Pius XI.

Seldom has a conclave excited more attention. The eyes of the world were on the Vatican. The nations were moving toward war. There were reports that Mussolini, at the instigation of his ally, Hitler, was trying to bring pressure to bear upon the Italian cardinals to elect someone who would be favorable to Fascism and Nazism. If the reports were true, Mussolini should have known better. No Pope could be favorable to a totalitarian form of government, and in any event the cardinals are men of outstanding character and could not be intimidated. Such stories, however, true or untrue, added to the general tension.

On the morning of March 1 as the conclave opened, a rainbow spanned the sky. Viewing it, people recalled that in times past God had used this as a sign of great things to come. They hoped that this would prove true once more.

Of the conclave itself little is known, for everyone who took part was sworn to strict secrecy. From here on we shall speak of the general rules that govern *all* conclaves with only a reference now and then to special conditions that applied in 1939.

The conclave was formerly a large room. Now it is an entire section of the Vatican Palace that an army of carpenters walls off temporarily from the rest of the building. Here, while the voting continues, the cardinals live, eat, and sleep, never emerging until a Pope has been elected. Each cardinal may take into the conclave a secretary and a servant. Besides these, there are cooks, waiters, guards, physicians, barbers, and workmen. (In 1939 the number of persons enclosed within the conclave was approximately 300). Every one of these persons takes an oath not to reveal what happens within the conclave.

The conclave is divided into apartments, each with three or four small rooms or cells. In each cell there is a crucifix, a bed, a table, and a few chairs. The cells are covered with cloth. Formerly the cloth was purple if the cardinals were raised to their rank by the last Pope, green if they were not. Now all are covered with green.

There is only one door, and once the conclave begins, the door remains locked except to admit a cardinal who is late in arriving. The door is guarded by members of the Chigi family, hereditary marshals of the conclave. It is not even possible to signal to anyone outside, for the windows are boarded up and glass doors are covered with paint. All telephone lines in this part of the Vatican are cut off. A revolving slide window through which food supplies, urgent messages, and letters are handed is the only means of communication with the outside world.

The government of the conclave is in the hands of the Camerlengo and the heads of the three cardinal orders. The latter succeed each other every three days in the order of their seniority. (In 1939 an American, Cardinal O'Connell, was head of the cardinal priests and had the honor of belonging to this group.) The Camerlengo assumes great importance at the time of the death of a Pope. At the same time the powers of the

Secretary of State cease altogether. Occasionally a Pope makes the Secretary of State the Camerlengo also. This was the case with Pope Pius XI who appointed Cardinal Pacelli to both positions.

Pope Pius X ruled that on the first day of the conclave the cardinals should assemble in the Pauline Chapel for the Mass of the cardinal dean and should receive Communion from his hands. Pope Pius XI changed this rule so that now each cardinal may celebrate a Mass.

On the morning of the second day the cardinals assemble in the Sistine Chapel, where the voting is to take place. Six lighted candles are on the altar on which rests the chalice to be used in voting. The Papal throne has been removed. Each cardinal has his own chair and over each chair is a baldachin. The baldachin is a sign of authority and signifies that while there is no Pope the cardinals are supreme. Before each chair is a writing desk. When the cardinals enter the chapel, they are accompanied by their secretaries and servants bearing portfolios and writing materials. Prayers are said by the Bishop Sacristan; the ballots are distributed, and then all leave except the cardinals, one of whom bolts the door.

The ballots are divided into three parts. At the top are the words *Ego Cardinalis* . . . (*I, Cardinal* . . .). The cardinal writes his name after these words, folds that part of the ballot, and seals it with wax. On the bottom part he writes a scriptural text. He also folds and seals this part. These parts will not be opened unless a Pope is elected by a very close vote. In this case the ballot of the Pope-elect is opened to show that he did not vote for himself. His ballot is located by the opening and the reading of the Scriptural texts. The cardinal elected must have a two-thirds majority without his own vote. In the center of the ballot are the words, *I choose as Sovereign Pontiff the Very Reverend Cardinal* . . . after which the cardinal fills in the name of his choice.

In turn each cardinal walks to the altar, kneels for a short prayer, rises, holds the ballot above the great gold chalice which is on a table there, and takes this oath: "I call to witness the Lord Christ, Who will be my Judge, that I am choosing the one who according to God I think ought to be elected." He then drops his ballot into the chalice, bows before the Cross, and returns to his throne.

Three of the cardinals are chosen by lot to be tellers. When all the cardinals have voted, one of the tellers takes the chalice and shakes it to mix the votes well. Another teller counts the votes and deposits them, one by one, in a second chalice. If there is not the same number of ballots as there are cardinals, the ballots are immediately burned and another vote taken. If the number is correct (as it always is), the tellers carry the chalice to a table in the center of the room and proceed to count the ballots. They open only the middle part of each ballot. As one of the tellers reads the names aloud, each cardinal follows the voting on slips of paper, printed with the names of all the cardinals. If no decision has been reached another ballot is taken immediately.

Four votes are taken every day, two in the morning and two in the evening, until the required majority is obtained. Each vote takes two or three hours. When no majority has been obtained, the ballots are mixed with wet straw and burned in a small stove which has a chimney extending up through a window. This makes black smoke, and when the people waiting outside see it they know that no decision has been reached. When they see white smoke — the ballots burned without the straw — they know that the Catholic Church has a new head.

When a cardinal has been elected, the cardinal dean asks him whether he will accept the election and by what name he wishes to be called. Usually the Pope-elect replies that he is sure it is the will of God that he takes up the heavy burden of the Papacy, and that therefore he accepts it. Then he selects his name.

Theoretically any faithful male Catholic may be elected Pope. Since 1522, however, the choice has always fallen on an Italian cardinal and on one who was present at the Conclave. Before that time some of the men who were elected were not even priests. It was necessary for them to be ordained and consecrated immediately.

As soon as the newly elected Pope accepts, the canopies of all the chairs except that of the Pope's are lowered. The new Pope is conducted to a neighboring room and clothed in Papal garments. The cardinals then advance and pay their first "obedience." They touch the Pope's foot with their lips, a sign of reverence. The Pope then appoints the new Camerlengo, who puts upon the Holy Father's finger the new Fisherman's Ring. After the cardinals have departed, the conclave is declared "open."

The coronation, which comes later, is in reality only a solemn blessing. The new Pope enjoys full jurisdiction from the moment of his election.

Chapter IV

"WE HAVE A POPE!"

A GREAT throng was waiting in the square in front of St. Peter's. All eyes were on the little chimney rising above the Sistine Chapel. It was toward evening on March 2, 1939.

For three weeks the great Catholic Church had been without a head. The beloved Pope Pius XI had died February 10, 1939. Now on Thursday, March 2, sixty-two cardinals from all parts of the world were meeting in the Sistine Chapel to select a new Supreme Pontiff. It was a critical period in the world's history. Who would lead the Catholic Church in the dark and stormy days that lay ahead?

The cardinals were cut off from all contact with the world outside. This was the second day of the conclave, the first day of balloting. The little chimney over the Sistine Chapel was the only indication of what was going on inside.

Twice little puffs of black smoke had risen from the chimney.

No decision.

When no cardinal receives the required two thirds of the votes, the ballots are mixed with wet straw and burned in a small stove. When a decision has been reached the ballots are burned without straw. This makes white smoke.

The crowd waited anxiously. In all parts of the world Catholics and non-Catholics alike sat tensely by their radios. Everyone recognized the great spiritual force of the Pope, and thousands not of his faith looked to him as the hope for a world gone mad.

Suddenly a puff of smoke appeared from the chimney. The crowd stirred excitedly. What color was the smoke? White! It was white! A thunderous cheer arose. "We have a Pope!" In many languages excited radio announcers told the story to the world. The name of the new Pope, they said, was unknown. He was being robed and would receive the obedience of the cardinals. In a few minutes he would appear on the balcony above St. Peter's and give his blessing to the city and to the world.

A white tapestry bearing the Papal coat of arms was hung from the railing of the balcony above the entrance to St. Peter's. The first cardinal deacon appeared on the balcony and stood before a microphone. Silence fell over the square. Millions sitting by their radios waited breathlessly for the announcement that was to follow.

The first cardinal deacon spoke in Latin. "I announce to you tidings of great joy. We have a Pope. He is Eugenio . . . ." At this, wild cheering burst from the crowd. No need to finish the name. Everyone knew and loved the former Papal Secretary of State. Everyone agreed that the perfect choice had been made. When the speaker could make himself heard, he concluded, "— Cardinal Pacelli. He will take the name Pius."

The bells of Rome pealed joyously. The people cheered, prayed, wept, embraced one another. Spontaneously they began to sing the Church's great hymn of triumph, *Te Deum*. Rarely has the world witnessed such a scene of unrestrained emotion.

Shadows were falling as the white-clad figure of the new Holy Father was seen approaching the balcony railing. The people in the square and millions by their radios fell to their knees. Pope Pius XII raised his right hand and made the Sign of the Cross. "In the Name of the Father, and of the Son, and of the Holy Ghost," he said.

This was the first time in history that a newly elected Pope had ever given his blessing to the world by radio. It was the first time in 272 years that a Papal Secretary of State had been elected Pope. It was the first time in centuries that a Pope had been elected on the first day of balloting.

Darkness fell, but a large part of the crowd remained in the square. Everywhere stood little groups of people discussing the momentous events of the day.

"God has been good to us," the people said. "He has given us a great and holy man to guide us through these troubled times."

Chapter V

"LONG LIVE THE POPE"

THE DAY on which the Coronation of a Pope takes place is a great day for Rome and for the Church. It is an occasion which does not ordinarily take place very often. Seventeen years elapsed between the Coronation of Pope Pius XI and that of Pope Pius XII.

At the Coronation the tiara, or triple crown, is placed on the head of the Pope. Little is known of the origin of the tiara, except that it is probably oriental. In the early centuries a single crown was used. Later, a second crown was added to show that the Pope had not only spiritual power but he also had the power to crown the head of the Holy Roman Empire. While the Popes lived at Avignon, a third crown was added. No one knows the reason for this. Perhaps it was to symbolize the fact that the Popes were the sovereigns of the Papal States.

Other explanations have been given for the three crowns: that they symbolize the Church militant, suffering, and triumphant; that they mean that the Pope is lawgiver, judge, and teacher.

There are centuries of tradition behind the coronation ceremonies just as there are behind almost everything that concerns the Pope. The coronation of Pope Pius XII was similar in most respects to the coronations of the past. In former years, however, only those actually in the Basilica knew what was taking place. In 1939 millions heard the ceremonies by means of radio.

The coronation of Pope Pius XII took place on Sunday, March 12, 1939. Eighty-five thousand persons crowded every corner of St. Peter's. Another half million stood in the piazza. Many of them had been there since midnight.

The pealing of silver trumpets from the dome of St. Peter's announced the beginning of the ceremonies. The throng within the church looked toward the main doors. A moment later a cross-bearer entered. This was the beginning of a brilliant procession consisting of guards and knights in gorgeous uniforms, richly robed bishops and cardinals, diplomats, representatives from 40 countries (including the United States), princes, and members of the Papal court. A murmur went up from the crowd as they beheld a glimpse of white at the end of the procession. They knew that the Holy Father was coming into view. A moment later they beheld him. He was seated on a portable throne (the *Sedia Gestatoria*). He was robed in white embroidered in gold, wore a jeweled stole around his neck, and had a gold miter on his head. The throne was carried by twelve footmen in red uniforms and was surrounded by noble guards and Swiss guards. At each side walked an attendant carrying a large fan made of white feathers.

The people burst into wild cheers when they beheld the Pontiff. *"Viva il Papa!"* they shouted, "Long live the Pope!" The Holy Father gave his blessing again and again as the procession proceeded through the nave toward the main altar. The choir sang the Papal hymn, "Thou Art Peter."

The procession stopped at the chapel of the Holy Trinity. There the Pope left his throne and knelt for a short while in adoration before the Blessed Sacrament.

In the midst of all this splendor a note of humility was struck. The procession was halted and a wisp of fiber was burned before the throne while the master of ceremonies said, *"Sancte Pater sic transit gloria mundi"* ("Holy Father, so passes the glory of the world"). This was repeated three times. The Church thinks it only proper to have colorful ceremonies when a new Vicar of Christ is being crowned, but she wants everyone, including the Pope, to remember that all such glory is passing, that we are on earth only to earn a place in eternity.

The procession halted near the main altar. The huge bronze statue of St. Peter which stands near by was clothed for the occasion in gold and scarlet robes and had a golden tiara on its head. Pope Pius left the *Sedia Gestatoria* and seated himself on a throne near the altar. The cardinals advanced and paid him their obedience.

Then Pope Pius began his coronation Mass. The first cardinal deacon placed over his shoulder the pallium, a small circular band of white wool. The pallium is worn only by the Pope and archbishops. For the Pope it is a sign of his authority; for the archbishops it is a sign that they share in the Pope's authority. The wool for the pallium is kept until it is needed in a golden casket near the tomb of St. Peter. There are many theories regarding the origin of the pallium. Some authorities believe it represents the mantle of Elias. When Elias was taken to heaven in a fiery chariot, his mantle fell off and rested on the shoulders of Eliseus. This was a sign that Eliseus was to take the place of Elias as prophet and lawgiver.

At the elevation of the Mass the silver trumpets sounded, and a deathlike silence descended over the church. Everyone fell to his knees — priests, bishops, cardinals, Swiss guards, visitors from foreign countries, the common people of Rome — all knelt humbly. As they beheld the Host raised in the Pope's hands, each said fervently in his own language the words which are said all over the world at this part of the Mass, "My Lord and my God."

After Mass the colorful procession re-formed to escort the Holy Father to the balcony overlooking the square. Here the crowning was to take place. This was to be the first time in 93 years that a Pope was to be crowned outside of St. Peter's.

Pope Pius IX, following the custom of centuries, was crowned there in 1846 at the beginning of his long reign. Then came the end of the temporal power of the Popes, and from then on the crowning took place inside the Basilica. This was the first coronation since the restoration of the temporal power and the old tradition was renewed.

A deafening roar, "Long live the Pope!" greeted the Holy Father's appearance on the balcony. The Pontiff seated himself on a gilded throne beneath a crimson canopy. A cardinal took the golden miter from his head and the first cardinal deacon lifted the gem-studded tiara from a red velvet cushion. A hush fell over the crowd. The big moment was at hand.

"Receive," said the first cardinal deacon, "the tiara adorned with three crowns, and know that thou art Father of Princes and Kings, Rector of the Universe, Vicar of our Saviour, Jesus Christ, who possessed the honor and the glory from century to century. Amen."*

With that he placed the tiara on the Pope's head.

The Holy Father, turning to the right and the left, gave his blessing "to the city and to the world" for the second time since his election. Then seating himself on his portable throne once more he was carried off the balcony and back into the Vatican.

The colorful five-hour ceremonies were over. The crowd slowly dispersed, and the Pope took up the heavy burden of his office. Within the short space of four weeks a Pope had died and been buried, and a new Pope had been elected and crowned. The Church now proceeded on its regular course.

---

* The full title of the Pope is: "Bishop of Rome; Vicar of Jesus Christ; Successor of St. Peter, the Prince of the Apostles; Supreme Pontiff of the Universal Church; Patriarch of the West; Primate of Italy; Archbishop and Metropolitan of the Province of Rome; Sovereign of the State of Vatican City."

The word *Pope* by which he is most often called is from the Italian word Papa, an affectionate term for father. "Pontiff" comes from the Latin word *Pontifex*, meaning bridge builder. In pagan times the Roman Pontiffs, or high priests, had charge of the bridges over the Tiber. The Pope often speaks of himself as "Servant of the Servants of God."

His Holiness Pope Pius XII.

Burton Holmes, from Galloway

The dome of St. Peter's as seen from the River Tiber.

St. Peter's Basilica.

International   A papal procession in St. Peter's.

International

The pope blessing the people from the balcony of St. Peter's.

International   The throng in the Piazza before St. Peter's on the occasion of the Pope's election in 1939.

Pope Pius XII celebrates Solemn Pontifical High Mass in St. Peter's.

Chapter VI

THE POPE WHO WISHED TO BE A PARISH PRIEST

WHEN MOST newly elected Popes assume their duties at the Vatican, they must accustom themselves to an entirely new life. They have visited the Vatican only for such matters as consistories and solemn ceremonies in St. Peter's. Now they must spend the greater part of their lives within the Vatican walls. The change is tremendous, and sometimes the adjustment is rather difficult.

This situation was not true for Pope Pius XII. He knew the Vatican well from earliest boyhood. He was reared almost in the shadow of it, and his father was the Consistorial Advocate of the Holy See as *his* father had been before *him*. Even as a boy, he probably heard Vatican affairs discussed morning, noon, and night. When he was ordained to the priesthood, instead of being assigned to a parish, he was given a position at the Vatican and there, except for twelve years spent in Germany and brief trips abroad, he has remained ever since. Eugenio Pacelli's training seemed to destine him to become the head of the Catholic Church.

The present Pontiff was born March 2, 1876, in Ponte, a suburb of Rome near the Tiber. His full name was Eugenio Maria Giuseppe Giovanni Pacelli. His father, Phillipo Pacelli, was a noted lawyer, dean of the Vatican bar, and the Consistorial Advocate. He also held a number of important offices in the city of Rome.

Eugenio and his elder brother Francesco attended a public school which was conducted by nuns. A classmate of Eugenio's who is now living in the United States says that even when he was a little boy, Eugenio was determined to become a priest. Despite the fact the family was well situated, Eugenio wore "simple, humble clothes to school and elsewhere — black short knickerbockers and black jacket and black shoes, to look as much like a priest as possible. A grave, quiet little boy he was, who plagued and baffled his teachers with searching questions about politics, economics, and religious history."

When he was ten or eleven, Eugenio volunteered to serve as an altar boy, and each daybreak he reported to the church to assist the priest in offering the sacrifice of the Mass.

Francesco wished to follow in the footsteps of his father and grandfather, and so he decided to study law. His ambition was fulfilled, for he later became Consistorial Advocate and played an important part in the negotiations leading up to the signing of the Lateran Treaty.

Eugenio, with his brilliant, discerning mind, would have made an excellent lawyer also, but a higher calling was in store for him. After finishing preparatory school, he entered the Capranica Seminary. He was able to remain there but a year, for his health was none too good. Because community life was too difficult for him he was allowed to live at home and go every day to the Pontifical Gregorian University. There he completed his studies for the priesthood.

Very rarely is a young man studying for the priesthood permitted to live at home. However, the authorities recognized in Eugenio exceptional qualities and felt that the Church would suffer a great loss if he were not allowed to continue his studies in spite of his poor health.

In 1899, when he was 24 years old, Father Pacelli celebrated his first Mass in the Church of Santa Maria in Vallicella at the tomb of the Apostle of Rome, St. Philip Neri.

Eugenio Pacelli's fondest wish was fulfilled. He was now a priest. He wanted nothing more than to be assigned to a parish where he could work among the people — talk with them, hear their confessions, make sick calls, teach Christian doctrine. But such was not to be. Eugenio's reputation as a great scholar had reached the ears of the higher authorities in the Church, and they had other plans for him.

Father Pacelli was appointed a substitute professor of law at the Roman seminary and also an apprentice in the Secretariate of State. The latter appointment was the beginning of his direct association with the Vatican which was to last for the remainder of his life. Very shortly afterward he was appointed titular professor of canon law in the Congregation of Extraordinary Ecclesiastical Affairs.

There is no record of Father Pacelli's reactions when he received these appointments, but he was no doubt greatly disappointed. Honors he did not desire — only the opportunity to serve his people as a parish priest. But priests, like soldiers, can only obey. Men who enter the priesthood are devoted to a lifetime of sacrifice, and the greatest sacrifice often comes in obeying the orders of their superiors.

Archbishop Gasparri, secretary of the Congregation of Extraordinary Ecclesiastical Affairs, was very much impressed by his young apprentice, and desired to have the full use of his time. With the consent of Pope Pius X and Cardinal Merry del Val, the Secretary of State, he requested Father Pacelli to turn in his resignation as professor and devote himself fully to the work of the Congregation. While in this position, Father Pacelli lived on the top floor of the Vatican Palace.

At the beginning of World War I, Pope Pius X died suddenly and was succeeded by Benedict XV. The new Pope appointed Gasparri, now a cardinal, Secretary of State, and Pacelli, now a monsignor, took the former's place as secretary of the Congregation of Extraordinary Ecclesiastical Affairs.

Pope Benedict did everything within his power to bring about the end of the war that was engulfing Europe, but he met with nothing but rebuffs and evasions from the leaders of the warring nations. Each side wished the complete destruction of the other side. A calm, impartial voice pleading for the brotherhood of man was lost amidst the din of clashing arms.

Although the nations did not listen to the Pontiff's appeals for peace, they did allow him to work for the exchange of prisoners. Monsignor Pacelli was in charge of this work, and the special staff, which he had for the purpose, worked day and night. Thousands of prisoners were exchanged, and many wounded soldiers from both sides were moved to Switzerland where they could recuperate. Church officials in all countries collected information on missing persons and prisoners of war. Families who had no word of missing sons for months often received this word through the Vatican. So, although the Vatican could not bring an end to the war, it did everything possible to lessen the suffering caused by it.

In 1917 Monsignor Pacelli was made Nuncio to Bavaria. Because of the importance of this post he was made the titular Archbishop of Sardia and was consecrated by Pope Benedict in the Sistine Chapel April 23, 1917.

Bavaria was a part of Germany, and it may be wondered why a Nuncio should be sent to only one section of a country. Germany, at that time, was a very young country and was made up of a confederation of German states. Each of these states had its own parliament and a large degree of independence. In a manner of speaking, Germany was a confederation of countries rather than a country in itself. Bavaria had been a Catholic kingdom before it had joined the German Reich and still had enough independence to be entitled to a Nuncio of its own. Archbishop Pacelli was to live in Munich, the capital of Bavaria.

Until this time Eugenio Pacelli had led a quiet scholarly life.

Even the work in the exchange of prisoners had been done from his office in the Vatican. Now he was to see some of the horrors of war at first hand. A few days after his consecration the new Nuncio was escorted through the Italian and German lines. In Munich he saw the dead and the maimed and the starving. He talked with the people of Munich and found that they longed for peace but could not have it.

In August, 1917, Pope Benedict launched the greatest of his peace moves. He proposed that the nations stop fighting and agree on a peace plan of seven points including the reduction of armaments and the settling of disputes by means of arbitration. It was the task of Archbishop Pacelli to present this plan to the German government. He traveled to Berlin where he spoke with both the chancellor and the Kaiser.

Kaiser Wilhelm was very much impressed by the Nuncio. "Pacelli is a distinguished, likable man, of high intelligence and excellent manners," he wrote in his memoirs, "the perfect pattern of an eminent prelate of the Catholic Church."

The Kaiser and the chancellor both seemed sympathetic toward the Pope's peace plan, and for a while it looked as if Archbishop Pacelli's efforts would meet with success. Later, however, the chancellor repudiated the plan, saying it had been prompted by Germany's enemies. So the war dragged on for another sixteen months and thousands of lives were needlessly sacrificed, and thousands of strong, healthy young men made cripples for life. A year later President Wilson announced his peace program with its famous Fourteen Points. Seven of the points were taken from the Pope's plan.

By the time the Armistice was signed, Germany was in a state of complete collapse. The population was hungry, bewildered, and completely disillusioned. For a while it looked as if Bolshevism would sweep the country. Many revolts broke out, especially in Munich. The government fled from Munich as did most of the diplomats. Only Archbishop Pacelli remained.

His was the only sane voice left in the city. From the pulpit of the Cathedral he preached constantly against Communism. It was true, he told the people, that their lot was an unfortunate one, but Communism would only make things many times as bad.

The Communists determined to still this powerful voice. A group of them, revolvers in hand, broke into his house and demanded to see him. Archbishop Pacelli came calmly down the broad staircase to meet them. He was dressed in the robes of office, a gold cross glittering on his breast. He was entirely without fear. The men who had come to kill him were so stunned that not one pulled a trigger. They stood there until he reached the bottom of the steps. He talked with them, analyzing their problems and pointing out the fallacies of Communism. One by one their revolvers dropped. A short time later the men left rather sheepishly. Afterward several of them returned to apologize.

The Communist threat finally abated in Germany and to Archbishop Pacelli goes no small amount of credit for this. He became the most popular diplomat in Munich and stayed there for another six years. In 1925 he was made the first Nuncio to Berlin, the capital of the new German republic. While there he concluded concordats with two German states, Prussia and Bavaria, and started negotiations for two more with Baden and Württemberg.

The great success of Archbishop Pacelli's work in Germany was due largely to his great knowledge of everything German. He speaks the language perfectly and is thoroughly familiar with the history, literature, and traditions of the country.

Through all these eventful years, Archbishop Pacelli looked forward to the day when he would be able to leave his ecclesiastical and diplomatic duties, relinquish his title as archbishop, and settle down to the life of a parish priest. In 1929 he was called to Rome to be made a cardinal, and then he knew that his hopes were blasted. This must have been one of the greatest disappointments of his life.

He took possession of his title in the Basilica of SS. John and Paul in Rome. During the sermon, which he preached on this occasion, he said that our Lord always requires sacrifices of His servants. In the early days of the Church, he said, many Christians had to sacrifice their lives for their faith. Today our Lord does not so often require from His servants sacrifices of blood, he declared, but He always requires from them sacrifices of the heart. Friends of the new cardinal, as they listened to the sermon, could not help reflecting upon the great sacrifice that he was making.

In 1930 Cardinal Pacelli was appointed Secretary of State to succeed Cardinal Gasparri who was retiring. The appointment was made by Pope Pius XI who had succeeded Pope Benedict XV in 1922 while Cardinal Pacelli was in Munich. One of the first duties of the new Secretary of State was to put into effect some of the provisions of the Lateran Treaty which had been signed the preceding year.

Two more honors came to Cardinal Pacelli not long after that. A month after he became Secretary of State he was made archpriest of St. Peter's, succeeding Cardinal Merry del Val who had just died. In 1934 he was made Camerlengo. Three high offices of the Church, which are usually entrusted to three different men, were now in the capable hands of Cardinal Pacelli.

The new Secretary of State was admirably fitted for his high office by his experience in the field of diplomacy. During the turbulent years that followed he performed the many duties of his office with wisdom, ability, and tact.

In 1934 Cardinal Pacelli was sent by the Holy Father as Papal Legate to the International Eucharistic Congress in Buenos Aires. He made an extensive tour of South America at that time and was everywhere received with great enthusiasm. The following year, at Lourdes, France, he represented Pope

Pius XI at the solemn ceremonies closing the Holy Year which commemorated the nineteenth centenary of the Redemption. In 1936 he opened the International Congress of the Catholic Press in Vatican City. At that time he spoke to the delegates in English, French, German, Spanish, Portuguese, and Latin.

In 1936 also came the eventful trip to the United States. This was the first time a Papal Secretary of State had ever visited here, and, as it turned out later, the first time a future Pope had ever come to this country.

In New York Cardinal Pacelli went to the top of the Empire State Building, went through Radio City, and did many of the other things which would be done by a typical tourist. He was so impressed by the Triborough Bridge that he halted the car three times to get out and inspect the construction.

From New York he went to Washington. There he revealed that, years before, he had been invited to become professor of Roman law at the Catholic University of America but had been told by the Pope that he was to remain in Rome. He visited the offices of the National Catholic Welfare Conference, the organization maintained by the bishops of the United States for the purpose of looking after Catholic interests and Catholic rights in this country. He visited Mount Vernon. He laid a wreath on the tomb of George Washington. He addressed a luncheon given in his honor by five hundred newspaper correspondents.

From Washington Cardinal Pacelli began his air journey across the United States in a plane especially chartered for the purpose. He carried a portable typewriter and wrote his speeches while in the air. He flew to Cleveland, to the University of Notre Dame, and to Chicago. At the latter city a mixup occurred, and the plane circled about for half an hour while the officials cleared the field. When the plane finally landed, the officials were apologetic. "No apologies," said the cardinal. "On the contrary I thank *you* for giving me a chance to catch up with my reading."

Everywhere he went he made friends with his slow warm smile, his quiet manner, and his eager interest in everything American. From Chicago he flew to St. Paul and then over the Rockies to San Francisco. In the latter city he was shown the two great bridges that span the bay, and Treasure Island which was being built in the bay for the coming Golden Gate Exposition. He flew on to Los Angeles and then commenced his trip back across the country.

On the way to St. Louis he saw Boulder Dam from the air. He made brief stops in Albuquerque, Amarillo, Wichita, and Kansas City. From St. Louis he flew to Cincinnati and then back to New York. On the way to New York he requested the pilot to fly several hundred miles out of the way so that he could see Niagara Falls from the air.

While in this country the cardinal had visited all four American cardinals and had talked with most of the American bishops. He had inspected many universities and seminaries. Always there were great crowds to greet him and to beg his blessing, which he gave freely. There were innumerable banquets, speeches, and receptions. He laid cornerstones, and graciously accepted a number of degrees. Through all this crowded schedule he never seemed to tire, and he was always ready to talk with people. At several airports he asked the police to let some children through the line so he could talk with them.

Just before sailing Cardinal Pacelli was the guest of President Roosevelt at the latter's home at Hyde Park, New York. This was the day after Roosevelt's re-election for a second term. "I was very anxious to meet the President," he said after the luncheon. "And I am very happy to have had the opportunity of seeing him and congratulating him on his re-election."

When he left the United States, a great crowd was at the wharf to see him off. America had taken the future Pope to its heart. Back in Vatican City, Cardinal Pacelli declared that his travels in the United States had left one of the deepest impressions of his life, and that the consoling memory of his visit to that great country and its people would forever be preserved in his heart.

By this time Pope Pius XI was in a very bad state of health, and it did not look as if he would live very long. He lived on for three more years, however, and continued to perform the exacting duties of his high office in those trying days when the world was edging closer and closer to the precipice of war. During these years Cardinal Pacelli continued in his office of Secretary of State, and he made several trips to various parts of Europe, representing the Pope at important ceremonies.

When the Holy Father died the whole world speculated on the question, "Who will be the next Pope?" Of the 62 cardinals, 28 were non-Italians, and so their election was thought to be rather unlikely. (The last non-Italian Pope was Adrian VI, a Dutchman, who died in 1523.) Of the 35 Italians, a number were more than 70 years old, and others were members of Religious Orders and so their choice, too, was rather unlikely. This left 18 who were regarded as possible choices. Cardinal Pacelli was among the 18, and people all over the world wondered whether he would be the next Pope. Because of his wide travels he was known to more people than any of the other cardinals. It was recalled, however, that only two Popes had ever held the office of Secretary of State and so, people thought, perhaps his chances were not so great.

As Camerlengo of the Holy Roman Church, Cardinal Pacelli performed his duties during the vacancy of the Holy See in a manner that won universal admiration.

When the announcement was made from the balcony of St. Peter's that the choice of the conclave was Eugenio Cardinal Pacelli, the enthusiasm of those standing in the square and those listening by the radio was unbounded. (See Chapter II.) No one could have been better suited to guide the Church through the troubled days that lay ahead. Americans had a special reason for being pleased. For the first time they could say of a Pope, "He visited our city"; "He came out on our playground and blessed us"; "He sat in that chair."

When the cardinals offered their first obedience just after the Pope's election, Cardinal O'Connell asked Pope Pius to give his blessing to all the people of America. At once the Holy Father replied, "With all my heart I bless them, and will always pray for them. They were so kind to me when I visited them."

As soon as he was elected, Pope Pius XII, as he chose to be called, began devoting all his energies to preventing the war that was threatening. Within 24 hours of his election he broadcast a plea to the world to enjoy peace of conscience, peace of family, and peace among nations. His voice was deeply moved as he declared that peace was his first wish as he mounted the throne of St. Peter.

For the next six months the Holy Father worked incessantly for the preservation of peace. Message after message was sent to the world's rulers. He begged them to settle their disputes without resorting to war. Audience after audience was held with those who could in any way be instrumental in preventing the war. On many nights he had only three hours' sleep. In all, he made seven public appeals for peace.

On August 24, Pope Pius broadcast a message *To Those in Power and Their Peoples,* saying: "Nothing is lost by peace, but everything may be lost by war. Men often retrace their steps and yield to negotiation. Once they begin discussing with good will and respect for mutual rights, they will discover that peaceful negotiations never stood in the way of a creditable issue. . . . We know the heart of every mother beats in response to ours. . . ."

A week later, on August 31, he sent messages to the Polish and German governments begging them not to start hostilities. The very next day the German invasion of Poland began, and World War II was under way.

The Pope adopted a policy of strict neutrality in the war, but this did not keep him from protesting when the rights of other neutrals were violated. He sent messages of sympathy to Poland, Norway, Denmark, Holland, Belgium, and Luxembourg. When Denmark and Norway were invaded, *Osservatore Romano* said, "The territorial neutrality of two more countries has been violated. Those who have defended the sacred rights of neutral countries against all and any cannot but regard with the deepest pain this sudden and dramatic extension of the theater of war."

Although unsuccessful in his efforts to prevent the war, the Holy Father worked to prevent its spreading. His efforts to keep Italy out of the war, his betrayal by Mussolini, and his subsequent persecution at the hands of Mussolini are told in Chapter XV.

The Holy Father endured all persecution with quiet resignation and continued to work for peace and the lessening of the suffering caused by the war. He laid down five points which he said must be the basis of a just peace. They are: (1) There must be no aggression; nations must respect each other's independence. (2) Minorities must not be oppressed. (3) No nation must be kept from sharing the riches of the earth. (4) Armament races must be avoided. (5) Religion must be free.

The Pope's experience in locating missing persons in World War I has stood him in good stead in World War II. He has established a new office under the Secretary of State, the Bureau of Information on War Prisoners. The Bureau was started in the early days of the war. Representatives of the Holy See in all countries at war gather the names and home addresses of war prisoners. These are sent to the Bureau which broadcasts to each country information about its soldiers who have been taken prisoner. A staff of more than 150 volunteer workers consisting of priests, sisters, and laymen handles the hundreds of inquiries that are received daily. The work of the Bureau has grown so rapidly that it has had to move to larger quarters. In the first four years of the war it located more than 40,000 missing soldiers.

In July, 1943, came the first bombing of Rome, followed shortly after by the "resignation" of Mussolini. (See Chapter XV.) There was another bombing in August, and once more Pope Pius went forth to comfort the panic-stricken populace.

In September came the announcement that Italy had surrendered to the Allies. The news was greeted with great jubilation both in Italy and in the Allied countries. The general impression seemed to be that this meant an end to the fighting in Italy. Italians were elated by the thought that at last peace was returning to their unhappy country.

However, bitter disillusionment followed when the Germans quickly seized all of northern and central Italy, including Rome; and Italians realized that the war was not over for them. Their country was to serve as a battleground between the allied American, British, and Canadian troops who had landed in the south and the Germans who were entrenching themselves farther north. People in the Allied countries realized that hard, bitter fighting lay ahead before they could take possession of the country that had surrendered to them.

Catholics the world over, and millions of non-Catholics as well, were horrified by the news that the Nazi legions had poured into Rome and that Vatican City was under their "protection." What would happen to the Holy Father and the Papal realm? Vatican City was a neutral country, but in the past the Nazis had won no great reputation as respecters of neutrality. They had, on the other hand, never made any secret of their enmity toward the Catholic Church.

The first reports to reach the outside world from Vatican City were a trifle reassuring. German soldiers had surrounded the tiny country but had not entered it. Any time they wished to do so, however, they could seize the Vatican with no opposition. Pope Pius had ordered the Swiss Guards not to resist in the event of an invasion.

Pope Pius XII was the new prisoner of the Vatican. He could not leave the Vatican without special permission from the Germans, and no one could see him without their permission. He was virtually cut off from all contact with his cardinals and the other Church officials. He could look out the windows of his apartment and see armed German soldiers patrolling the streets.

No one could have been better fitted to meet this trying situation. Pope Pius's great serenity, his experience in the field of diplomacy, his knowledge of the German character, and his great personal courage were qualities that were to his advantage. Facing German guns was nothing new to him. He had faced them that day back in Munich when the German Communists had come to kill him and had stayed to talk with him.

On at least three occasions the Pontiff defied the Nazis during their occupation of Rome. He stood upon his rights as the head of a neutral nation and refused to yield to them the refugees who had fled into Vatican City. When the Germans held a group of Roman Jews for ransom, the Holy Father expressed his disapproval of the act by giving gold for their release. When the Germans "suggested" to him that it might be better if he were to leave Vatican City and go to Liechtenstein or some other place where they would be better able to "protect" him, he replied that he would not leave the Vatican "while I am alive."

On the night of November 5, a plane dropped four bombs on Vatican City. The Mosaic Studio and the Governor's Palace were damaged, and windows in St. Peter's and other buildings were shattered. The world was indignant at the bombing of this tiny neutral state. After extensive investigation by General Dwight D. Eisenhower, our state department announced that "beyond any doubt" the plane that dropped the bombs did not belong to the United Nations.

The Allies fought their way closer to Rome, and the Germans seemed determined to defend the city to the end. It appeared to be virtually certain that Rome would once more become the bloody battleground it had been so often in the past. People everywhere prayed for the safety of the Holy Father. They prayed, too, that Rome and Vatican City be spared any further ravages of war.

On June 2, 1944, the Holy Father addressed the members of the College of Cardinals who had come to visit him on the feast of his patron, St. Eugenius. By this time the Allies were within sight of Rome, and the sounds of battle could be plainly heard within the confines of the Vatican. The Pope warned that "whoever dared raise a hand against Rome would be guilty of matricide in the eyes of the civilized world." He also made a plea to the world for a just peace.

Two days later Rome fell to the Allies almost without a battle. The prayers of the world had been answered. Never had belligerents been so solicitous of a city. The Germans had always defended their other positions to the very last and had destroyed them before they retired, but they left Rome intact. The Allies, aside from a few bombings of the railroad yards, had withheld their fire from the city. In view of the widespread fears that had been held for the safety of the city, its safe deliverance seemed little short of a miracle.

Early the next morning thousands of Romans and many Allied soldiers gathered in St. Peter's Square to cheer the Holy Father. Twice the Pope appeared at his office window in response to the cheering. That evening he came to the balcony of St. Peter's. Between 250,000 and 500,000 persons stood in the square and in the new avenue leading to it. American jeeps and command cars were parked on the steps of the Basilica. More jeeps were on the fringe of the crowd a quarter of a mile away.

"We have trembled for the fate of the city," the Pontiff said to the throng. "We must give thanks to God for the favors we have received. Rome has been spared. This day will go down in the annals of Rome."

He said a prayer of thanksgiving and then, as the immense crowd knelt before him, gave his blessing "to the city and to the world."

No man in the world has as many responsibilities as the Holy Father, and no man works longer hours than he. The working day of the Pope lasts from 6 a.m. until midnight with a few intermissions for meals and recreation. He never sleeps more than six hours out of twenty-four.

The Holy Father rises at 6 a.m. on the dot. He dresses, shaves with his electric razor, and then exercises for about ten minutes in his private gymnasium. Next he says Mass and afterward spends half an hour in prayer. Then he has his breakfast, which consists of coffee, bread, and butter.

About nine o'clock he goes to work in the library on the second floor of the Papal Palace. There he goes over the mail with his chamberlain, a layman, Giovanni Stefanori. Later the Papal Secretary of State appears for a talk. This talk usually lasts an hour or so. The work of the Secretary of State is, of course, very familiar to Pope Pius XII. Private and public audiences follow. In the course of the private audiences the Holy Father hears reports on the condition of the Church in all of the various countries. His visitors are nearly always astonished at his great fund of knowledge and his quickness in grasping the most complicated problems.

Public audiences are held at least once a week, usually more often. On these occasions he is on his feet for five hours at a time, giving everyone his ring to kiss, speaking to many, blessing all. Never during all this time does he lose his serenity or show the slightest sign of strain. He frequently sees 2000 persons during the course of a day.

About 2 p.m. the Holy Father takes time for lunch. A typical lunch consists of soup, veal, greens, cheese, fruit, and watered white wine. Then he goes for a walk in the Vatican gardens which are closed to visitors at this time. If the day happens to be rainy he enjoys the walk even more than on other days, for walking in the rain is one of his favorite pastimes.

After lunch he returns to the library for more work. He often spends the afternoon at his typewriter composing speeches, letters, and special communications.

At 8:30 Pope Pius eats his dinner, which usually consists of eggs, vegetables, cheese, and fruit, and then he goes back to work until midnight. Occasionally in the evening he listens to an hour or two of phonograph records. He prefers the operas of Wagner.

The Pope has a summer home at Castelgandolfo, ten miles from Rome, but he has not been there since the war started. Despite the intense heat of a Roman summer he prefers at the present time to remain in Vatican City, close to the center of everything.

Pope Pius XII is tall and slender. He is utterly fearless, and one of the world's most learned men. From a distance, he seems reserved, but persons who talk with him find him exceedingly friendly. He will rank among the greatest statesmen of all times. He is pious, humble, kind, and has a deep concern for the souls of which he is chief shepherd.

The Church could not have chosen a more capable leader to guide her through these troubled times than this man whose greatest ambition was to be a parish priest.

PART III
The Government of the Church

Chapter VII

THE COLLEGE OF CARDINALS

WHAT ARE cardinals? There are many answers to this question. They are the counselors of the Pope. They are the men who elect the Pope. They are often called Princes of the Church. Collectively they are called the Senate of the Church and also the Sacred College.

All of these answers are true, but they do not go to the bottom of the matter. What are cardinals *really*? What makes them cardinals? *Cardinals, with the exception of the six cardinal bishops, are the honorary parish priests of Rome.*

"How can this be?" one may ask. "There are cardinals in the United States, thousands of miles from Rome. How do they fit into this definition?"

The answer is that each of the cardinals in other countries has a *titulary* church in Rome. This means that he has the *title* to a church in Rome even though he may not see it for years at a time. He appoints a vicar to manage the affairs of the church for him. Actually, however, the cardinal is the pastor.

There are three orders of cardinals: cardinal priests, cardinal deacons, and cardinal bishops.

Why are the cardinals so divided? How does a cardinal priest differ from a cardinal bishop or a cardinal deacon?

The best way to answer these questions is to go back into history and to trace briefly the development of the College of Cardinals.

The word *cardinal* comes from the Latin word *cardo* which means hinge. In the beginning a cardinal was any priest who was permanently attached to a church. In time only the priests at the largest and most important churches were called cardinals. Not all the priests attached to these churches were called cardinals, however — only the first priest or pastor.

By the end of the fifth century there were about 28 churches in Rome that had cardinal priests. The Pope, as Bishop of Rome, bestowed various duties on these cardinals and often asked their assistance in running the affairs of the Church. He often called meetings of the cardinal priests. The oldest of them was called the archpresbyter and assisted the Pope at all solemn functions.

Rome was not the only diocese that had cardinals. The pastors of important churches in the dioceses of Constantinople, Magdenburg, Milan, Ravenna, Naples, Sens, Trier, and Cologne were also called by this title. Their bishops called them into conference just as the Bishop of Rome called his cardinals. We see, therefore, that originally the cardinal priests were those priests who were attached to important churches in a number of dioceses. Later, however, one of the Popes ruled that only Rome could have cardinals, and so today we find that cardinal priests are the pastors of important churches in Rome. Now what about cardinal deacons?

In the early days of the Church, Rome was divided into seven regions. Each of these regions was presided over by a deacon. His principal duties were to assist the poor and to find out as much as possible about the acts of the martyrs. The deacons often assisted the Pope at various functions. The priests who were closely associated with the Pope were called cardinals so it is not surprising that soon the deacons too were called by this name. This was the beginning of the order of cardinal deacons. Gradually the seven regions disappeared but the Pope continued to call upon the deacons. In time the number was increased from 7 to 14. Today the pastors of some churches in Rome are cardinal deacons; the pastors of others are cardinal priests.

Knowing the origin of the other two orders, one could almost guess the origin of the cardinal bishops.

As the Church continued to grow, the Pope began frequently to call upon the bishops of other dioceses for assistance. By this time the term cardinal was used to denote someone very close to the Pope, and so it was not long before it was applied to these bishops. Today the bishops of the six dioceses nearest Rome are the cardinal bishops. The cardinal dean is always the Bishop of Ostia.

Therefore, we see that cardinals have always been those who were closely associated with the Popes. In the first two centuries after the death of our Lord, the Church was very small and was constantly being persecuted. There was no need for a large organization. When the persecutions ceased and the Church began to spread to all parts of the known world, it was necessary for the Pope to have a group of men who could advise him and who could help him administer the affairs of the Church. It is only natural that these men should have a special rank and a special title.

In 1059 the cardinals suddenly became more important than they had ever been before. From the earliest times the members of the Roman diocese have had the privilege of electing their own bishops. Because the Bishop of Rome is also the Pope, they had the additional very great privilege of selecting the head of the Universal Church. At one time the people themselves elected the Pope. Later the privilege was restricted to the priests of Rome. Since the cardinals were the foremost priests, they naturally had an important voice in the election. In 1059,

Pope Nicholas II gave them the power of electing the Pope, but their choice had to be approved by the rest of the clergy and the people of Rome.

By this decree the cardinal bishops were to meet and select the men they considered best fitted for the Papacy. Then all the cardinals were to gather and take part in the election. Finally, the consent of the rest of the clergy and of the people had to be obtained. Although the cardinals now had a much greater voice in the election, the idea of the people taking part in the choosing of a Pope was still kept. Finally, in 1139, the cardinals alone were given the right to select a Pope, and in 1179 the rule was established that the Pope must be chosen by a two-thirds majority of the cardinals present. These rules are still in force. The conclave, or meeting of the cardinals within an enclosed place for the election of the Pope, originated, as we already have seen, in a proclamation of Pope Gregory X in 1274.

From all this it can be seen that the cardinals, when in conclave, are not the representatives of the Universal Church gathered to elect a Supreme Pontiff. Technically, they are the priests of the Diocese of Rome, plus a few neighboring bishops, meeting to elect their bishop. The Pope is head of the Church because he is Bishop of Rome; he is not the Bishop of Rome because he is the Pope. The reason for this is that Christ Himself appointed St. Peter the head of His Church, and the Bishop of Rome is the successor to St. Peter. If there were no College of Cardinals, the privilege of electing a Pope would not belong to the bishops of the world. It would belong to the priests and possibly to the people of Rome.

Since the development of the College of Cardinals was so gradual, the rank of its members was rather uncertain at first. Gradually cardinal bishops were looked upon as ranking higher than other bishops, and later they also outranked archbishops and patriarchs. In time cardinal priests and cardinal deacons also came to rank higher than any other members of the Church except the Pope himself.

As the College of Cardinals gained in power and prestige, the order of cardinal priests came to include archbishops and bishops. Today tradition decrees that *only* archbishops and bishops may be cardinal priests. Occasionally a member of the hierarchy is a cardinal deacon. Priests and those in minor orders may also be cardinal deacons.

In monarchies cardinals are equal in rank to royalty. Even many republics give them a place above ambassadors.

At the present time it is possible for the Sacred College to consist of six cardinal bishops, fifty cardinal priests, and fourteen cardinal deacons — seventy in all. This number is rarely reached. There were 62 cardinals at the time Pope Pius XI died.

The robes of a cardinal are scarlet. He has a biretta and a skullcap of the same color. If he is a member of a religious order, however, he may continue to wear a cassock the color of his religious habit. A large low-crowned red hat is also a part of the cardinal's dress; it is not worn but is carried behind him in certain religious ceremonies. He wears a ring set with sapphires.

Cardinals are appointed by the Pope. Cardinal priests and cardinal bishops must be at least thirty years of age. A cardinal deacon must have entered his twenty-second year. A cardinal deacon must receive his deacon's orders, if he does not already have them, within a year after his appointment.

The creation of cardinals takes place in a meeting called the secret consistory. Only the Pope and the cardinals attend this meeting. The Holy Father names those whom he intends to raise to the rank of cardinal and asks those assembled for their opinion. They remove their caps as a sign of consent. "By the authority of God Almighty," says the Pope, "and that of the Apostles Peter and Paul, and our own, we create the following cardinals . . ." Then he names them.

In the afternoon of the same day the newly created cardinals, if they live in Rome, meet in the Pope's apartments, in the ante-chamber of which the scarlet skullcaps are handed to them. Then the scarlet biretta is placed on the head of each by the Pope. In the next public consistory the Pope gives to each cardinal his red hat.

At the beginning of the next secret consistory the ceremony known as the "opening of the mouth" takes place. At the end of the consistory the "closing of the mouth" takes place. Thus are symbolized the duties of the cardinals to keep the secrets of their office and to give counsel to the Pope. At this consistory the ring is given to each new cardinal and at the same time the "title" or church that shall thenceforth be his.

If the newly created cardinal lives outside of Italy, the skullcap is brought to him by one of the noble guards and the biretta by a special messenger. In Austria, Spain, and Portugal the biretta is usually bestowed on the cardinal by the head of the government. In such cases the recipient promises that within a year he will go to Rome for the remaining ceremonies.

At the end of the Secret Consistory at which the Pope has nominated the new cardinals, he sometimes says, "We have also created . . . (here he names a number) cardinals whose names we retain *in pectore* to be proclaimed at our own discretion."

The cardinals thus nominated are called cardinals *in pectore* or *in petto*. The former is the Latin form, the latter the Italian. The words may be translated to mean "in the heart." They are so called because for a time their names remain locked within the heart of the Pope. Cardinals *in petto* cannot assume any of the duties of cardinals until the Pope has announced their names publicly. Should he die before he reveals their names, they never receive the rank of cardinal. When the public announcement does take place, however, their seniority dates back to the time they were created *in petto,* and they rank higher than those who were named later.

The principal duty of the cardinals is to act as counselors of the Pope. For this reason, many of them are obliged to live in Rome and cannot leave without special permission. They share in the government of the Church through the consistories, the Roman Congregations, the Roman Tribunals, the five Offices of the Curia, and various ecclesiastical commissions. It is different, of course, with the Cardinals who live in other countries.

The consistories are meetings of the Pope and the cardinals. There are three kinds of consistories: secret, public, and semi-public. At the secret consistories everyone is excluded but the Pope and the cardinals. Anyone having any business before the consistory appears at the public one. The semipublic ones are attended by bishops as well as cardinals. Much of the important business of the Church is transacted at the consistories, such as the appointment of bishops, archbishops, and patriarchs, and their transfer from one see to another. It is at the consistories that new dioceses are established and old ones divided. All the details for such matters have been prepared ahead of time in the Congregation of the Consistory.

The Congregations, the Tribunals, and the Offices of the Curia will be treated in succeeding chapters.

Cardinals have many duties and many privileges. Their very highest privilege comes after the death of the Pope when, assembled in solemn conclave, they have the honor of filling the vacancy in the highest office in the world.

Chapter VIII

THE CONGREGATIONS AND THE TRIBUNALS

EVERYONE WHO has taken a course in civics knows what
a vast thing is the government of the United States. In a high
school or college course which lasts a semester, or even a year,
you barely scratch the surface. You learn the three divisions
of the government — executive, legislative, and judicial — and
you learn the powers and duties of the President, Congress, and
the Supreme Court. But you cannot possibly know the workings
of the hundreds of bureaus within the ten departments of the
executive branch. You may, if you are a very apt student,
know the names of all the Congressional committees, but you
can't tell the exact duties of each. You may know all the lower
federal courts, but in all probability you can't tell just which
cases are handled by each court or which cases may be appealed.
The government of a country containing 130,000,000 persons
is so detailed that only those who have devoted their lives to
the study of it can be entirely familiar with it.

The government of the Catholic Church is likewise a vast
affair. There are more than 300,000,000 Catholics, and they
are living in every country of the world. The Pope is the head
of the Universal Church, but in order to govern it he needs
a great amount of help. If it is impossible in an entire course
in civics to understand a great deal about the government of
the United States, it is even more impossible, in the space of

a few short chapters, to explain fully the government of the Catholic Church. We can, however, take a quick, over-all glance at it and learn something of its principal divisions.

The Roman Curia is the name given to all the departments and ministries that form the government of the Church. It consists of the Roman Congregations, the Roman Tribunals, and the five Offices of the Curia.

There are twelve Roman Congregations. They are:

1. Congregation of the Holy Office
2. Congregation of the Consistory
3. Congregation on the Discipline of the Sacraments
4. Congregation of the Council
5. Congregation of Religious
6. Congregation of Propaganda of the Faith
7. Congregation of the Sacred Rites
8. Congregation of the Eastern Church
9. Congregation of Ceremonies
10. Congregation of Extraordinary Ecclesiastical Affairs
11. Congregation of Seminaries, Universities, and Studies
12. Congregation of the Fabric of St. Peter's

The Roman Tribunals are:

1. The Sacred Penitentiaria (or Penitentiary)
2. The Sacred Roman Rota
3. The Apostolic Signatura

The Offices of the Curia are:

1. The Apostolic Chancery
2. The Apostolic Datary
3. The Apostolic Camera
4. The Secretariate of State
5. The Secretariate of Briefs to Princes and of Latin Letters

In this chapter we shall consider briefly the twelve Congregations and the three Tribunals. The five Offices will be left to a later chapter.

The Roman Congregations might be compared somewhat to our own departments of government, and the cardinals at their heads correspond roughly to our cabinet members. At the head of each Congregation is a cardinal prefect appointed by the Pope. The only exceptions are the Congregation of the Holy Office, the Congregation of the Consistory, and the Congregation of the Eastern Church. The Pope himself is prefect of these. Besides the prefect there are several other cardinals and many clerks, experts, and consultants whose duty it is to study questions as they arise and report their findings to the cardinals for their decisions.

The Roman Congregations prepare the administrative work of the Pope. The Holy Father has the final say in everything, but he pays careful attention to the advice of the cardinals who are the members of the Congregations.

The Congregation of the Holy Office is the oldest and one of the most important of all the Congregations. Its purpose is to defend Catholic teachings on matters of faith or morals. The Holy Office deals with all matters that, directly or indirectly, concern faith or morals; it judges heresy and offenses that lead to the suspicion of heresy. It applies the punishments that are incurred by heretics, schismatics, and the like. It is the only congregation that has judicial power. The Pope himself is head of the Holy Office.

One of the numerous duties of this Congregation is to pass on the so-called miracles which occur in many parts of the world. The Church moves very slowly in such matters and pronounces that a miracle has taken place only after the most painstaking investigation, which in most cases takes a number of years to complete.

In 1917 the Congregation of the Index was abolished and the Holy Office took over the work formerly done by this

Congregation. This branch of the Holy Office censures and condemns books that it considers dangerous to faith or morals. Its list of condemned books is called the Index, and no Catholic may read any books on the list without securing special permission.

The Congregation of the Consistory has much in common with the Holy Office and has the same head, the Pope. It prepares the work of the consistories. Among many other duties it plans the creation of new dioceses and it nominates bishops.

The Congregation of the Discipline of the Sacraments deals with the laws regarding all sacraments. Two of its three divisions are devoted to Matrimony. Priests desiring to celebrate Mass in a private chapel, on an ocean liner, or any other place not ordinarily authorized, send their requests to this Congregation. It can also grant requests to say Mass before dawn or after noon if the reasons are urgent enough. Recently it granted American Army chaplains the privilege of saying evening Mass. It can dispense anyone (except priests who say Holy Mass) from the Eucharistic fast if the necessity seems great enough.

The Congregation of the Council was founded in 1563 to carry out the decisions of the Council of Trent. Although the Council no longer exists, the Congregation does. Parish priests, Sodalities, beneficent societies, and stipends for Masses, are under its jurisdiction. So are fasting, abstinence, and the observance of feast days.

The Congregation of the Council has jurisdiction over the "Holy House" of Loretto, which was formerly cared for by a special congregation. Within the Basilica at Loretto is a small house in which, tradition says, the Holy Family lived in Nazareth. It was said to have been brought to Italy by the angels in 1291. The story has never been pronounced authentic; nevertheless many pious pilgrims go there to pay respect to the Blessed Virgin, and many miracles have taken place there.

The Congregation of Religious has jurisdiction over religious orders. It alone has the power to approve new orders and their constitutions and to approve the modifications of old ones.

The Congregation of Propaganda of the Faith has as its purpose the spread of the Roman Catholic Church to every part of the world. All the missionary countries are under its jurisdiction. Its power is so vast that the cardinal who presides over it is called the "Red Pope." Until 1908 the United States was included within its jurisdiction although it had long ceased to be a missionary country.

The Congregation of the Sacred Rites has two functions. Its first function is to direct the liturgy of the Latin Church. By liturgy is meant the ceremonies or rites which are used by the Church on all occasions. By the Latin Church is meant that section of the Church — by far the largest — which uses Latin in its ceremonies.

The other function of this Congregation is deciding on beatifications and canonizations. This is an enormous undertaking. Before the Church decides that a person is definitely in heaven and worthy of the prayers of the faithful, vast masses of evidence must be studied. The most interesting official in this process is the promoter of the faith, often called the "devil's advocate." It is his duty to gather all evidence that might cast doubt on the candidate's sanctity. If despite all the evidence of the devil's advocate the Church decides that the person is worthy to be beatified and canonized, there can be no doubt about the matter. Usually the investigation lasts several lifetimes, sometimes hundreds of years.

The Congregation of the Eastern Church is new, dating only from 1917. The Pope himself is prefect of it. This congregation deals with a section of the Church that is little known to most American Catholics. We usually think of the entire Church as having the same ceremonies and using the same language, Latin. There are, however, approximately fourteen rites besides the Latin. The people who belong to these rites hear Mass said in Greek, Armenian, Russian, Arabic, Rumanian, and several other languages. Their ceremonies, while fundamentally the same as those of the Latin rite, differ greatly in nonessential details. The people who belong to these rites are Catholics in perfectly good standing, and the Pope is their head. They are all under the jurisdiction of the Congregation of the Eastern Church.

The Congregation of Ceremonies has charge of the etiquette and customs of the Papal court. Its prefect is the Bishop of Ostia, dean of the Sacred College.

The Congregation of Extraordinary Ecclesiastical Affairs is unusual in that besides being a Congregation it is also a section of one of the five Offices of the Curia, the Secretariate of State. It has as its head the Secretary of State, although he is not called a prefect. It has no fixed duties and considers all matters that the Pope and the Secretary of State refer to it.

The Congregation of Seminaries, Universities, and Studies has had its present title only since 1915. Before that it was the Congregation of Studies. Originally it had charge of institutions of higher learning in the Papal States. Now it has charge of such institutions all over the world, not excepting those run by religious orders.

The Congregation of the Fabric of St. Peter's has charge of the immense Basilica of St. Peter and of the Studio of Mosaics. About $40,000 a year is spent on the maintenance of the Basilica and the number of workmen assigned to it is approximately 400.

These, then, are the Congregations which in their daily, weekly, or monthly meetings conduct a large part of the business of the Church. Now for a brief look at the Tribunals, or courts.

The Sacred Penitentiaria dates back to the twelfth century when Pope Innocent II reserved for himself "absolution for crimes against the clergy." At that time priests were often the victims of armed attacks. As the number of these attacks increased the Pope found it necessary to set up a special court to examine the requests for absolution that came from all parts of the world. The tribunal is still primarily a court of mercy. It can grant dispensation from certain rules and absolution from sin. It deals with all matters of conscience submitted to the judgment of the Holy See.

The head of this tribunal is the Cardinal Penitentiary. He assists the Pope at the hour of his death, reciting the customary prayers for the dying. Mention will be made in a later chapter of the confessionals in St. Peter's and of the rods with which the confessors touch the heads of the penitents. It is the members of the Sacred Penitentiary who occupy these confessionals and use these rods. They are also found in two other basilicas in Rome: St. John Lateran and St. Mary Major.

The Sacred Roman Rota is known to the general public as the court which decides upon marriage annulment cases. This is only part of its work, however. Criminal and civil cases are also tried there.

The Apostolic Signatura is often called the Supreme Court of the Catholic Church. It hears chiefly cases that have been appealed from the Rota. The Holy Father may from time to time refer other cases to it, and it is occasionally called upon to review decisions of the Congregations.

We have now considered the work of the twelve Roman Congregations and the three Roman Tribunals. There still remain the five Offices of the Curia. These we shall consider next.

Chapter IX

THE POPE'S ASSISTANT

THE CARDINAL Secretary of State has often been called the Pope's assistant. He has also been called the Prime Minister of the Church. Next to the Holy Father, whose will he serves, he is the most powerful official of the Church. Of all the cardinals who compose the Sacred College, he alone lives at the Vatican. He alone sees the Holy Father every day of the year. The office of Secretary of State becomes vacant after the death of each Supreme Pontiff, and the new Pope appoints his own confidential adviser.

The Secretary of State presides over one of the five Offices of the Curia, *the Secretariate of State.* This also includes, as we have seen, one of the Congregations, the Congregation of Extraordinary Ecclesiastical Affairs.

The Secretariate deals primarily with the relations between the Holy See and the various governments of the world. At the present time thirty-eight countries are represented at the Vatican by a minister or an ambassador. (The United States is not listed among these thirty-eight because Myron C. Taylor is the President's personal representative and does not have diplomatic status. The relations between the United States and the Vatican are discussed in a separate chapter.) The Vatican has thirty-eight representatives abroad, not including apostolic delegates. These representatives are called Papal Nuncios and deal directly with the governments of the countries to which they are sent.

Many Nuncios later become cardinals. The late Pope Pius XI was Papal Nuncio to Poland before he was made a cardinal. Pope Pius XII was Papal Nuncio to Munich and Berlin before he became a cardinal. Both had adventures in these posts which show that a Nuncio's life is not always an unexciting one. Pope Pius XI, then Monsignor Ratti, was Nuncio to Poland when a Bolshevik army from Russia marched on Warsaw, the Polish capital. When all the other diplomats fled, Monsignor Ratti stayed on. His prayers, encouragement, and courageous example so inspired the Poles that they gathered together the remnants of their retreating army, turned about and defeated a Russian army many times as large. The battle saved Europe from Communism.

When Pope Pius XII, then Archbishop Pacelli, was Nuncio to Bavaria, German Communists, as we have seen in an earlier chapter, threatened his life, pointing loaded revolvers at his breast.

Besides the Nuncios, who are the same as ministers or ambassadors, the Holy See has another group of representatives called the apostolic delegates. They represent the Holy See with the bishops of the countries to which they are sent, but not with the civil authorities. They are sent to countries which have not established diplomatic relations with the Vatican. The United States has an apostolic delegate.

There is a third class of representatives called the Papal Legates. They are temporary representatives and are appointed for special occasions such as Eucharistic Congresses, or to discuss certain questions with heads of governments.

Concordats, or agreements between the Holy See and civil governments, come within the jurisdiction of the Secretariate of State. Under Pope Pius XI the Holy See made more concordats than had ever before been made in a similar length of time. In all of them the Vatican was given the right to name bishops without interference. In most of them the countries promised to respect the Church's rights in such matters as education and marriage.

The origin of the office of Secretary of State goes far back into history. The Pope has always had need of a confidential assistant and for many years this assistant was taken from his own family and was called the "Cardinal Nephew." Enemies of the Church bitterly attacked this idea. "Why should a Pope favor a member of his own family in this way?" they asked. The Pope, however, felt that a member of his own family, a person whom he knew very well, would make the best confidential adviser. Most of the cardinal nephews were conscientious and worked very hard. One of them, Charles Borromeo, cardinal nephew to Pope Pius IV, has been canonized.

As the relations with other governments increased, the office of Secretary of State was created. The cardinal nephew, however, took precedence over the Secretary of State. In 1692 the office of cardinal nephew was abolished, and for a while there was question as to whether his duties would fall to the Secretary of State or to the Camerlengo. Today it is the Secretary of State who is the Pope's principal assistant and confidential adviser while the Pope is alive, and the Camerlengo assumes great importance after the death of a Pope. Cardinal Pacelli, the present Pope Pius XII, was both Secretary of State and Camerlengo.

The office of Secretary of State has been occupied by a long list of distinguished churchmen. In 1907 Douglas Sladen, a non-Catholic, writing of Cardinal Merry del Val, then Secretary of State, said:

"The Cardinal Secretary needs encyclopedic knowledge and almost superhuman intuition and tact; gifts with which Cardinal Merry del Val is richly blessed. He has to pass from subject to subject without losing the threads. . . . No Prime Minister in Europe is so accessible. . . . He is allowed the widest discretion, because one of his most important functions is to save the Pope from unnecessary business. . . . There are few people who know so much of the religious affairs of all countries as Cardinal Merry del Val. . . .

"His time for book reading is necessarily limited, but the way he keeps up with newspapers is extraordinary. . . . He has . . . an army of correspondents and confidential agents and has need for them all. . . . He is obliged to make personal enemies by his decisions, and, in addition, all the enemies of the Church are his enemies."

Cardinal Merry del Val was succeeded by Cardinal Gasparri who was named Secretary of State by Pope Benedict XV in the first year of World War I. This was a very trying period for the Church. Both sides wished the support of the Pope, and he had to steer a neutral course. The Pontiff and Cardinal Gasparri labored valiantly to bring an end to the war. The cardinal had the rare distinction of serving under two Popes, for Pope Pius XI also named him Cardinal Secretary. It was during the latter reign that the Lateran Treaty was signed after several years of negotiations. Cardinal Gasparri played an outstanding role in these negotiations. After the signing of the Treaty, Cardinal Gasparri retired with the highest honors the Pope and the King of Italy could give him. He was recognized as one of the foremost statesmen of the century.

Cardinal Pacelli became the next Secretary of State and performed his work with distinction. It was while he held this office that he made his famous visit to the United States. Upon the death of Pope Pius XI, he was elected Pope. One of his first acts was to appoint as Secretary of State, Luigi Cardinal Maglione (mal yone e).

Cardinal Maglione has had a long and distinguished career in the diplomatic service of the Church. A few years after his ordination in 1901 he was admitted as an apprentice to the Congregation of Extraordinary Ecclesiastical Affairs. In 1918 he was sent to Switzerland as a representative of the Holy See. After he was there for two years, he was raised to the rank of Nuncio. In 1926 he was sent to France as Nuncio — a difficult post which he filled most capably. The French Government awarded him the Grand Cross of the Legion of Honor. In 1935 he was made a cardinal by Pope Pius XI, and at the same time was recalled to Rome to serve as head of the Congregation of the Council.

Cardinal Maglione and Pope Pius XII were classmates at Capranica College in Rome when they studied for the priesthood. Both have been trained in diplomacy, and both have a firsthand knowledge of conditions in Europe. The management of relations between the Holy See and the governments of the world could not be in better hands.

Although conducting relations with foreign governments is the chief business of the Secretariate of State, there is a section of the Office called the Chancellery of Briefs. Briefs are short papal letters and are usually used to confer honors. The Orders of Saint Sylvester, Saint Gregory, and Pius IX — titles of nobility — are given to eminent Catholic laymen through the means of a brief. Briefs were formerly stamped with the Fisherman's Ring, but today a rubber stamp is used.

The Secretariate of State is but one of the five Offices of the Curia. Before leaving the subject of the government of the Church let us glance at the other four offices.

The Apostolic Chancery sends out bulls, which are papal letters used for such solemn matters as condemning a heresy, ratifying a concordat, canonizing a saint, establishing a diocese, or erecting a university. The word *bull* comes from the Latin *bullere*, to boil. A bulla was a circular plate of metal which resembled a bubble. The term came to be applied to the lead seal with which Papal documents were signed and later to the documents themselves. Today the lead seal is usually left off and a rubber stamp used instead. The cardinal who is the head of the Chancery is called the chancellor.

The Apostolic Datary gives out benefices. That is, this office appoints those who are to fill positions to which regular amounts of revenue are attached.

The Apostolic Camera was formerly one of the most important offices in the Church. It was the central board of finance in the Papal States. When the Papal States were abolished, the Camera lost most of its importance. Today the chief source of revenue for the Vatican is the Peter's Pence collection, and that is in the hands of another body. Today the chief duty of the Camera is to administer the property of the Holy See when the Papal throne is vacant. The head of this Office is the Camerlengo who, as we have seen, assumes great importance after the death of the Pope.

The Secretariate of Briefs to Princes and of Latin Letters is entirely separate from the Secretariate of State but is similar to it in many ways. The Secretary of Briefs to Princes prepares the letters that the Holy Father sends to royal rulers, presidents of republics, and bishops. The Secretary of Latin Letters writes the letters of less importance.

Both of these secretaries are consulted by the Pope before the publication of his encyclicals. An encyclical is a letter sent by the Pope to the bishops of the world, or to the bishops of a certain country, who, in turn, communicate its contents to all the faithful within their jurisdiction. It is a pronouncement upon an important topic — such as marriage, Communism, the rights of the workingman, the education of youth.

Because encyclicals are so important the utmost care must be taken in their writing. They are written in Latin, and so the secretaries must have an excellent knowledge of this language. They must also have a very extensive knowledge of conditions in the world and of the subjects covered in the encyclicals.

The more we know about the men who form the government of the Catholic Church the more we realize that in all the world there are none more gifted and learned.

Chapter X

THE UNITED STATES AND THE VATICAN

A FEW days before Christmas, 1939, when World War II was just four months old, President Roosevelt announced that he was sending a personal representative to the Vatican. He was to assist Pope Pius XII in relieving suffering, bringing about peace, and establishing a better world order.

On the day following the President's announcement, the Holy Father, in a Christmas message to the cardinals, expressed his gratitude to the President and said he hoped that the appointment of a personal representative would some day result in the creation of a permanent American mission to the Vatican.

The President's announcement caused a storm of protest in anti-Catholic circles in the United States. "This violates our time-honored principle of separation of Church and State," cried some. "Our political and religious freedom is being threatened," they said. They begged President Roosevelt to reconsider his decision. The President replied very politely but declined to change his mind. These accusations were, of course, sheer nonsense. At one time the United States had a minister to the Papal States and certainly no restrictions on our religious and political liberty came about as a result.

While Rome was the capital of the Papal States, the United States had a representative there for seventy years, from 1797 to 1867. For most of this time the representative was a consul, but for twenty years we had an accredited diplomat in Rome.

It is interesting to note that the first time an American body had occasion to recognize the Pope as a sovereign was in 1757, nineteen years before the United States came into being. At that time England and Prussia were aligned against France, Russia, Austria, Poland, and Sweden in the Seven Years' War, which was called the French and Indian War on this side of the Atlantic. Many privately owned British vessels, called privateers, were commissioned to prey on enemy shipping — a sort of legalized piracy. In 1757 two British privateers brought into New York a captured vessel bearing the Papal flag. The captain of the ship brought suit in an Admiralty Court in New York, claiming damages for illegal seizure. The court ruled that since the ship was carrying the flag of a neutral nation, the Papal States, it had been seized illegally. The court awarded the captain a verdict of 1,645 pounds.

From 1797 to 1848 the American representative in Rome was a consul. A consul is a man who looks after the commercial interests of the country that he is representing. He is not a member of the diplomatic service. The first consul was John B. Sartori, a native of Rome. The second, Felix Cicognani, also a Roman, bore the same family name as the present Apostolic Delegate to the United States, His Excellency the Most Reverend Amleto Giovanni Cicognani. After these two, all the other consuls were Americans.

In 1846 Pope Pius IX was elected, and his election was very popular in the United States. He was regarded as a liberal and had indicated that he would give the people a greater voice in the government of the Papal States. Immediately after his election he released all political prisoners and relaxed the censorship of the press. He demanded the withdrawal of the Austrians from Italy and urged the unification of Italy. At that time Italy was divided into a number of small countries of which the Papal States was one. Most of these countries were dominated by Austria.

Americans cheered these actions of Pope Pius IX. They were

heartily in favor of any government that they considered democratic, and they believed in a United Italy free from Austrian influence. Newspapers urged that we establish diplomatic relations with the Papal States to show our sympathy with the policies of the Pope. Public demonstrations in favor of this were held in many American cities. The legislatures of New York and Louisiana passed resolutions urging the action. From Rome came information that the Pope would welcome a diplomat from the United States.

In 1847 in his message to Congress President Polk said, "The Secretary of State has submitted an estimate to defray the expense of opening diplomatic relations with the Papal States. The interesting political events now in progress in these States, as well as a just regard to our commercial interests, have in my opinion rendered such a measure highly expedient."

The recommendation brought about a long discussion in both houses of Congress, but the appropriation was finally passed by large majorities, 137 to 15 in the House of Representatives, 36 to 7 in the Senate.

On April 1, 1848, the state department announced the appointment of Jacob L. Martin as first charge d'affaires to represent the United States at the court of Pius IX. This choice was very popular with the press and the people.

Mr. Martin's instructions were specific. He was to deal with the Pope as a civil ruler, not as the head of the Catholic Church. This was partly to appease anti-Catholic sentiment, for in those days, too, the cry was raised that this move was a threat to the principle of separation of Church and State. He was to promote political good will and was especially instructed to gather and report to the state department "full and accurate information" about commercial relations between the United States and the Papal States. He was to suggest measures for increasing commerce between the two countries.

Mr. Martin arrived in Rome in August, presented his credentials to the Papal Secretary of State, and was cordially received in audience by the Pope. Twenty days later he died after a sudden attack of fever. In his brief term of office he had sent two interesting and lengthy reports to the state department.

President Polk appointed Lewis Cass, Jr., to succeed Jacob Martin, and the Senate confirmed the appointment by a vote of 28 to 24. In 1853 the diplomatic post in Rome was raised in rank to that of minister resident, and Mr. Cass served as first minister. He remained in the post for ten years and was succeeded by John B. Stockton, who was appointed by President Buchanan in 1858. The next three ministers were appointed by Abraham Lincoln. They were Alexander W. Randall in 1861, Richard M. Blatchford in 1862, and Rufus King in 1863. King served until Congress declined to appropriate any more money for the post in 1867.

The twenty years during which the United States had diplomatic relations with the Papal States were stormy ones in both countries. Pope Pius IX was beset by enemies both within and without his country, and finally almost all his territory was taken away from him. In this country the terrible Civil War was fought.

The forces of "liberalism" were on the rampage in Europe. Pope Pius IX was a liberal and had a sincere desire to do everything he could to help the people of Italy and to give them a greater voice in the government. He realized, however, that complete self-government cannot be thrust upon a people all at once. They must be educated to their responsibilities.

The extremists were not satisfied with what they called the minor reforms of Pope Pius IX. They caused uprisings in Rome and forced the Pope to grant a constitution. Even then they were not satisfied. The uprisings grew in intensity. The Pope's prime minister, Count Rossi, was stabbed to death; one of his prelates was shot. Finally the Pope was forced to flee for his life. A republic was set up with Mazzini at its head.

Many Americans, mistaking radicalism for democracy, wanted our country to recognize Mazzini's republic. They criticized our diplomat for not presenting his credentials to Mazzini. Our country, however, steadfastly refused to recognize the upstart government as did the nations of Europe.

The events which followed in Rome proved that the Pope was right when he maintained that democracy could not be thrust upon a people. The republic of Mazzini was frightfully mismanaged. Outrage followed outrage. Even many of the people who had put Mazzini into power became disgusted with his government. The Pope appealed for aid, and France sent troops to restore order in the Papal States. The republic came to an end and Pope Pius IX returned to Rome April 12, 1850. Now he was no longer prepared to grant liberal reforms. Italy was not ready for democracy.

The American Civil War presented another delicate diplomatic situation. Jefferson Davis, president of the Confederate States, sent a delegation to Europe to solicit the support of the Papal States and the other countries of Europe. The delegation brought a personal letter to Pope Pius IX from Mr. Davis. The Holy Father sent a reply addressed to Mr. Davis as the president of the Confederate States. The Pope also sent letters to the archbishops of New York and of New Orleans asking them to do what they could to bring about an end to the war.

Both these actions brought many protests from this side of the Atlantic. Many Northerners said that by his letter to Jefferson Davis, the Pope was recognizing the Confederacy. Persons in both the North and the South said that by the letters to the archbishops, the Pope was taking sides.

The American minister made inquiries in regard to both these cases. In his report to the state department he said that ordinary diplomatic courtesy required that the Pope reply to Jefferson Davis' letter. The fact that the letter was addressed to him as President did not imply formal recognition of the Confederacy. The letter to the two archbishops was written as head of the Catholic Church. In the letters the Pope asked Catholics in both the North and the South to work for the end of the war that was causing such bloodshed. The fact that he wrote to an archbishop in the North and one in the South should have been proof enough that he was not taking sides. He desired only to see peace established.

Despite these situations the relations between the two countries were very cordial. All five of the men who represented the United States spoke of their friendly reception by the Pope and the officials of his government. All their business was transacted promptly and without misunderstandings. The fact that we had a representative in Rome did not affect the separation of Church and State in this country.

Very little was left of the Papal States in 1867 when Congress decided not to appropriate any more money for the mission. In 1860 the forces of Victor Emmanuel had taken all of the Pope's possessions except the city of Rome and a little bit of surrounding territory. In 1870 Rome itself was taken, and the Papal States were a thing of the past.

Our period of diplomatic relations with the Papal States lasted for almost twenty years. In that time there were seven Presidents of the United States, but there was only one Pope; Pope Pius IX had one of the longest reigns in history.

Why did Congress refuse to appropriate the money for the post? There were a number of reasons. Anti-Catholic feeling certainly played its part; ever since the founding of the United States there has been a certain minority bitterly opposed to anything and everything Catholic. This group is always quick to seize upon any pretext for discrediting the Church.

It was charged in Congress that the American Presbyterian Church had been ordered outside the walls of Rome. This was entirely untrue, but doubtless influenced a number of votes. It was also said that since the Pope had no minister in the

United States, we should not send one to Rome. Some Congressmen thought that a minister was not needed in a country so small. By this time, it must be remembered, the Pope's territory had shrunk to the city of Rome.

There was much sympathy in the United States for a united Italy. This had been one of the reasons for establishing diplomatic relations with the Pope in the first place. At that time it looked as if Italy might be united under the Holy Father. Now the forces of Victor Emmanuel held most of Italy, and the Pope seemed to be in the way of a united Italy. Therefore many Congressmen thought we should close diplomatic relations with the Pope so that the way would be cleared for recognizing Victor Emanuel.

Finally, and perhaps this was the biggest reason of all, there was a feud between Congress and President Andrew Johnson. Johnson, who became President upon the assassination of Lincoln, faced a Congress so hostile that it was ready to refuse everything he asked. This was the Congress that impeached and almost convicted Johnson. The mere fact that the President asked for an appropriation for the mission in Rome was reason enough for Congress to refuse.

The action of Congress was very embarrassing to Rufus King, the minister at that time. His office had not been abolished, only his salary. He continued to serve several months without pay and then left Rome January 1, 1868. He was our last representative at the Vatican for a period of 72 years.

"It was to be regretted," says Dr. Leo Francis Stock in his book *U. S. Ministers to the Papal States,* "that the United States was not more candid in terminating the mission. . . .

"Even the official letter of recall was not sent King, so he could not take formal leave of the Papal authorities. It was not a courteous exit nor a dignified ending to this chapter of American diplomacy. Small wonder King was given to understand that the Holy Father felt hurt 'by the hasty and apparently groundless action of Congress,' and thought it 'an unkind and ungenerous return for the good will' he had always manifested toward the American Government and its people."

Two years later the temporal power of the Pope came to an end (see Chapter XIII) and the question of sending a representative to the Vatican was seldom raised in this country. In 1929, when the temporal power was restored, many persons asked if we should not again send a representative of some kind to the Holy See. That nothing was done about it for ten years was due chiefly to two reasons. The first, which can never be left out entirely, was anti-Catholic sentiment in the United States. The other was the fact that the tiny state of Vatican City would never have any commercial relations with the United States. The Papal States was a good-sized country. Vatican City, as a nation, is insignificant.

The election of Pope Pius XII in 1939 was similar in many respects to the election of Pope Pius IX in 1846. In both cases the choice was extremely popular in the United States. The present Pope's intense desire for peace struck a responsive chord in American hearts. Also, he had traveled in the United States when he was Secretary of State and had won the friendship and respect of the American people.

When the coronation of the new Pope took place, President Roosevelt sent Joseph P. Kennedy, then ambassador to Great Britain, to represent him at the ceremonies. This was the first time in history that a President had ever done such a thing.

Then on December 23 of the same year the President announced that he was sending Myron C. Taylor to be his personal representative at the Vatican. In the letter announcing the appointment the President said to the Holy Father that Christmas, 1939, would be a sad one because of the war. He believed, however, that a better world order, for which people long, is coming, and that all persons — both in religion and government — who desire peace and a just settlement of the problem which it will bring should work together in close co-operation. Therefore, the President wrote, it would give him great satisfaction to send his personal representative to the Holy Father to assist in bringing about the ends for which both the Pope and the President are striving.

"To you," he concluded, "whom I have the privilege of calling a good friend and an old friend, I send my personal greetings this Christmas season."

Myron C. Taylor, the man whom President Roosevelt selected as his representative to the Holy See, is a wealthy and distinguished lawyer, banker, and steel manufacturer of Chicago. He had often been called upon by the President to consider problems of relief and unemployment. He is an Episcopalian.

The appointment did not mean that diplomatic relations had been re-established with the Vatican. To bring this about both Congress and the Holy See would have to take action. Mr. Taylor has the privileges but not the title of ambassador.

It was at the end of February, 1940, when Mr. Taylor arrived at Vatican City. With Papal and American flags fluttering from their three cars, he and his secretary and an escort of Vatican attendants drove through the bronze gates. Accompanied by a guard of honor, the Americans climbed the two flights of marble stairs to the Papal apartments. An official ushered them into the small throne room where the Holy Father gave them what they afterwards called, "a very warm, dignified, and friendly welcome." Mr. Taylor presented the Pope with a letter from the President. Then they chatted for some time in English, and the Pope sent a warm greeting to President Roosevelt and a blessing to the American people.

After a period of 72 years the United States once more had a representative at the Vatican.

PART IV
History of the Vatican

Chapter XI

THE VATICAN IN EARLY TIMES

HOW DID the Vatican become the center of the Christian World?

Rome was far removed from the scene of our Lord's labors, and the Vatican was a marshy district across the river from Rome. Does it not seem strange that a desolate region on the outskirts of a city several thousand miles from the places associated with our Lord's life should become the center of the Church which He founded?

It was St. Peter who made Rome the center of the Christian world. After the Descent of the Holy Ghost upon the Apostles, St. Peter traveled extensively making thousands of converts everywhere he went. He met constant persecution and often his life was in danger. Once when he was in prison and sentenced to death, he was miraculously released by an angel. No complete record has been made of his travels, but it is known that he arrived in Rome about A.D. 42 and became that city's first Bishop.

There were other bishops in other cities, but all acknowledged Peter as the first among them. His word was always accepted as final. Had not our Lord Himself before His ascent into heaven, made Peter the head of His Church?

St. Peter was put to death in Rome sometime near A.D. 67 and St. Linus became the second Bishop of Rome. The Catholics of the world then looked to St. Linus as their supreme leader, for, as Bishop of Rome, he was the successor to St. Peter. Thus from the time of St. Peter, the Bishop of Rome has always been the head of the Catholic Church.

We see, then, that Rome became the center of the Christian world because St. Peter established himself there and died there. But why the Vatican? That is a longer story —

*   *   *

No one knows the origin of the name Vatican. Some think it was the site of an ancient Etruscan town named Vaticum. (The Etruscans lived in central Italy before the Romans.) Others think it was named after Vaetes, an ancient seer or prophet. Many other theories have been advanced. One guess is probably as good as another.

There was a hill in the middle of the district and the land around it was largely swamp. Cicero, Tacitus, and many others tell us that the district was known for its unhealthful air; and Martial said, "If you drink Vatican wine, you drink poison."

The area could not have been entirely swamp, however, for it was here that Lucius Quinctius Cincinnatus is said to have had his little farm of four acres. The story of Cincinnatus is one of the first legends to be associated with the Vatican district.

Rome, so the story goes, was engaged in a war with the Aequians and was meeting defeat after defeat. In desperation, the government decided that a dictator was necessary and Cincinnatus was the unanimous choice.

The envoys sent to summon Cincinnatus found him plowing on his farm. When he heard the news, he left his farm and rushed into the city. There he was received with great acclaim as the man of the hour, the only one who could save Rome from her peril. Under his direction the Aequians were defeated in sixteen days. Cincinnatus, his task performed, relinquished his title and happily returned to his farm.

For centuries there were no important buildings in this quarter. The first one to be erected was a circus or race track, which was built by the emperor Caligula a few years after the death of our Lord. Many sporting events were held there. Later some changes were made in it by Nero, and today it is usually referred to as the Circus of Nero. Occasionally it is called the Circus of Caligula. In this circus the first persecution of the Christians took place. Nero looked on gleefully while Christians were burned at the stake, torn to pieces by lions, or put to death in a hundred other horrible ways.

St. Peter was crucified in the circus. Tradition says that at his own request he was crucified upside down because he felt he was not worthy to die as his Saviour had. He was buried in a vault near the scene of his execution. St. Anacletus, the third Pope, built a little oratory or chapel over the vault. This chapel may be said to have been the beginning of the Vatican as we know it. For a while the body was removed from the vault, but it was restored to its original resting place by Constantine.

Three centuries of persecution came to an end with the reign of the Emperor Constantine. Constantine marching against his enemy Maxentius saw in the heavens a flaming cross. Over it he and his army could read the words, "In this sign you will conquer." Constantine adopted the cross as his standard and won a crushing victory over Maxentius. Partly because of this and partly because of his natural inclinations Constantine ordered that the persecutions of the Christians come to an end at once, and he did all in his power to help them. The emperor himself was baptized just before he died.

At the request of Pope Sylvester, Constantine began the erection of a great church on the spot where St. Peter was buried. The work was begun in A.D. 306, and Constantine is said to have labored with his own hands, carrying twelve basket-loads of earth in honor of the twelve Apostles. Part of the wall of the old circus was used in the construction of the church. The main altar was erected just over the tomb of the Apostle. Pope Sylvester dedicated the Basilica on November 18, 324.

This church, the first Basilica* of St. Peter, was about half the size of the present church, but it was the largest in the world at that time and the most magnificent. It stood until 1506, more than a thousand years. It would take many pages to describe the magnificence of this church. It was, in many ways, superior to the present Basilica.

For centuries the Popes did not live at the Vatican. They resided at the Lateran Palace which Constantine had built for them on the other side of Rome. The Lateran Basilica was the Cathedral Church, and, it remains so to this day. They frequently visited the Vatican Basilica, however, for special ceremonies. They soon found that it was necessary to have buildings at the Basilica so that they and their escorts would have places to dress, and occasionally places to spend the night. The priests in charge of the Basilica and the guardians of St. Peter's tomb also had to have lodgings. These were the first of many buildings to cluster about St. Peter's and to form what we today call the Vatican. Later, houses were erected for the pilgrims who flocked to St. Peter's tomb. By 752 there were four monasteries in the district and a number of mausoleums.

Rome was invaded many times by enemies of the Christian religion, and the Vatican suffered in every one of these invasions. One of the worst of these occurred in 846 when the fierce Saracens, coming from Sicily which they had conquered some years before, landed at the mouth of the River Tiber and swept up toward Rome. The city of Rome, secure behind its wall, resisted, but the Vatican fell into their hands. The treas-

---

* A basilica is a type of building that originated in the East and was brought to Rome. It is rectangular in shape and is divided into a nave and two side aisles. The early Christians adopted this type of architecture, and many of the foremost churches of Europe are of the basilica type.

ures of centuries were pillaged. What could not be carried away was broken. When the Saracens were finally driven out, even the altars and doors had disappeared.

Pope Leo IV saw that Rome had been saved because of the strong wall which surrounded it. He determined that the Vatican should have similar protection. Between 848 and 852 he enclosed the Vatican with a great wall forty feet in height and containing twenty-four towers. A section of this famous Leonine Wall, including two towers, still stands in the Vatican Gardens near the radio station. The land surrounded by the wall was called the Leonine City, and for more than a thousand years it remained separate from the city of Rome. Finally, in the sixteenth century, Pope Sixtus V placed it under the jurisdiction of the officials of Rome.

During the centuries that followed, the Vatican continued to grow. In the thirteenth century Nicholas III began the erection of a great palace and secured land for the Vatican Gardens. The Vatican of today was beginning to take form.

The Popes continued to live at the Lateran Palace, but more and more important functions came to be performed at the Vatican. In 1303 the conclave that elected Pope Benedict XI was held there. This was the first of fifty-two conclaves that have been held at the Vatican.

Clement V, elected in 1305, decided to live in Avignon, France, instead of in Rome. There were two reasons for this decision. First, there were bitter fights between the various factions in Rome, and life there had become intolerable. Second, Pope Clement was French and he desired to live in his native country. From 1305 to 1377, no Pope resided permanently in Rome. Urban V returned in 1367 but left again in 1370. Then in 1377 Pope Gregory XI, mainly because of the urging of St. Catherine of Siena, returned to Rome and that city once more became the home of the Popes.

The sights that greeted the eyes of Pope Urban V when he

arrived in Rome were enough to make him weep. Everything was in ruins. Houses were falling apart. There were great gaping holes in the streets. The population had dwindled to almost nothing. All authority had disappeared, and the citizens had to barricade themselves behind the walls of their houses to protect themselves from the bandits who boldly prowled the almost deserted streets.

The Lateran Palace, which had been the home of the Popes since the time of Constantine, had been destroyed by fire, so when Urban V was in Rome, the Vatican became the ordinary Papal residence. The latter place had been so neglected that it had become a wilderness. Wolves stalked through the gardens. Chapels, museums, and apartments were caving in and had to be completely overhauled. The work of repairing the damage extended through the reigns of the Popes succeeding Urban V.

Thus it was that in the fourteenth century the Vatican, despite its deplorable condition, took on new importance. It was no longer merely a shrine to St. Peter. It became the home of the Father of Christendom. It has remained so ever since.

Chapter XII

THE VATICAN IN RECENT TIMES

NICHOLAS V, who was Pope in the middle of the fifteenth century, is considered the father of the modern Vatican. He moved the entire government of the Church to the Vatican. He showed great genius as an architect and drew up plans for a new Basilica. His plans included the great square or piazza in front of the church. Work on the new Basilica started during his pontificate but had not progressed very far when he died. He started the beautiful Vatican Gardens over which visitors exclaim today. Most of the Papal Palace was constructed under his direction. It was he, also, who began the Vatican library which has grown to be one of the greatest in the world. The Vatican, as it appears today, is largely the result of the plans of this Pope who lived five hundred years ago.

Pope Sixtus IV, elected in 1471, had been a poor Franciscan friar, so poor that on the day he was made a cardinal, he had no lodging for the night. Although poor in worldly goods, he was endowed with a brilliant mind and a wonderful imagination. He did much to leave his imprint on the Vatican. His outstanding work is the Sistine Chapel, named in his honor. A great number of artists worked on the chapel during his reign. Among them are such famous names as Pinturicchio, Perugino, Botticelli, and Ghirlandajo. The Pope himself directed these artists, and their work stands to this day a monument to his memory. Pope Sixtus IV also greatly enlarged the library. He did very little work on the new Basilica. The Basilica built by Constantine continued to be used during his reign.

The three Popes who succeeded Sixtus IV did very little to change the Vatican. Then Pope Julius II, who was elected in 1503, decided to continue the work on the new Basilica. He called in Bramante, the outstanding architect of the day, to draw the plans for the church. The twelve-century-old Basilica of Constantine was torn down within a few weeks.

It was also Pope Julius II who ordered Michelangelo to paint the ceiling of the Sistine Chapel. Michelangelo undertook the work with a will. He himself put up the scaffolding which was to be his home for so many months. For two years the artist lay on his back painting his magnificent picture of the Creation. All day long he lay there, his head thrown back, his neck stretched, his veins swelling, and his face and beard spotted with the paint that dripped from his brush.

At the end of the two years Michelangelo descended. His neck was so stiff that he could not see his feet, and to read he had to hold the paper over his head. Carpenters speedily took down the scaffolding so that the painting could be seen. Pope Julius and the other spectators gasped at the grandeur of the work. They saluted Michelangelo as one of the greatest artists of all ages.

While Michelangelo was painting the ceiling of the Sistine Chapel, another famous artist, Raphael, was decorating the Papal apartments. The work of these and other great artists make the Vatican one of the world's greatest storehouses of art treasures.

Later (1535-1541) Michelangelo painted the Last Judgment over the altar of the Sistine Chapel. This took six years. Meanwhile Bramante, who had died in 1520, had been succeeded by other architects who changed his original plans for the Basilica. In 1547 Michelangelo was named architect. He returned as much as possible to Bramante's original plans and designed the famous dome, the most beautiful in the world. He did not live to see the dome completed. He died at the age of eighty-nine, having served the Popes as artist, architect, and sculptor.

The huge column of granite or "needle" as it is called, which stands in the middle of St. Peter's Square, was placed there September 10, 1586. It is the oldest object in Vatican City, older than St. Peter's tomb. It once stood in Nero's circus near the spot where St. Peter was crucified. Pope Sixtus V determined that it should have the place of honor in the square.

A large crowd watched in silence as the great column, weighing many tons, was slowly lowered upon a long platform. The people had been cautioned to be silent, for any noise might startle the workmen who had to devote every bit of attention to the task at hand. A false move might prove disastrous. On thirteen rollers the needle was moved the short distance from the ancient circus to the middle of the square. Then the work of raising it commenced. Eight winches, turned by sixteen horses and eight men, had to strain at the ropes before the needle budged. Then for one terrible moment it appeared that the great mass of granite would break the ropes, fall, and shatter to bits. The crowd gazed in horrified silence.

Suddenly the silence was shattered by a workman shouting "Wet the ropes!" This was done. The cables contracted, the winches moved, and the needle continued to rise into place. A great sigh of relief went up from the people massed in the square.

Work on the famous colonnade that surrounds the Square was commenced under Pope Alexander VII who reigned from 1655 to 1667. It was designed by Giovanni Bernini.

From that time until the beginning of the reign of Pope Pius XI no important changes were made in the Vatican. Many of the buildings, the library for example, were enlarged and improved. Many art treasures were added to the collections.

Under Pope Pius XI many changes were made. Telephone

and telegraph systems were installed. Marconi himself put in the radio station. Railroad tracks were laid and a little white stone station was built. The post office was enlarged. Automobiles were introduced. In short, the ancient institution was completely modernized. But that is the subject of another chapter.

Chapter XIII

THE POPE'S KINGDOM

BESIDES BEING the spiritual ruler of 330,000,000 Catholics throughout the world, the Pope is also the ruler of a tiny nation, Vatican City. This nation of 1000 persons is the smallest country in the world. At a leisurely pace a person can walk across it in fifteen minutes. There was a time, however, when the Pope was the ruler of a large part of central Italy. He was a king as well as the Supreme Pontiff.

How did the Pope come into possession of this territory? The story begins with Constantine, the emperor who put an end to the persecution of the Christians. For centuries Rome had been the capital of the greatest empire the world had ever known. But in 330 Constantine decided to move the capital to Byzantium in what is now Turkey. The city was renamed Constantinople in his honor.

Later it was found that the vast Roman Empire could not be ruled from Constantinople as well as it could from Rome. In 395 it was split into two parts, the Eastern Empire and the Western Empire. The Emperor of the East lived in Constantinople. The Emperor of the West chose to live in Ravenna rather than in Rome. When Rome was no longer the capital, the city was left without any high political officials, and the people looked more and more to the Pope as their leader and protector.

In 452 Attila and his horde of Huns swept into northern

Italy, murdering and pillaging as they went. The emperor was powerless to stop them and begged Pope Leo the Great to help him save the country. Leo visited the barbarian leader and obtained from him the promise that he would leave Italy and make peace with the emperor.

Three years later, in 455, Rome was captured by the Vandals and the same Pope Leo obtained from Genseric, their leader, the promise that he would not injure the city or take the lives of any of its inhabitants. No wonder the people looked more and more to the Pope as their protector! The Pope did not seek temporal leadership; it was thrust upon him. With the Western Empire decaying someone had to befriend the people.

The Western Empire came to an end in 476, and Rome was again ruled from Constantinople. For two centuries the Popes were loyal supporters of the emperors. In 692, however, when Emperor Justinian II unjustly ordered the arrest of Pope Sergius II, the people rushed to the Pope's rescue and forced the emperor's representatives to flee back to Constantinople.

In 752 the Lombards threatened Rome and Ravenna. The emperor was powerless to protect these cities, and so the Pope raised an army which succeeded in defending them. Two years later the same Lombards under King Aistulf seized portions of central Italy, and this time the Pope's army was not strong enough to drive them out. At the emperor's request, Pope Stephen II crossed the Alps into France to secure the help of Pepin the Short, King of the Franks. In the summer of 754 Pepin marched into Italy at the head of a great army. King Aistulf shut himself up in his palace and sued for peace. He promised Pepin that he would restore the conquered provinces to the Pope. Pepin put the provinces under the rule of the Pope and said that he would act as the protector of the Pope's domain.

This act was called the *Donation* of Pepin. It was the beginning of the Papal States and of the temporal power of the Pope. The Papal States endured from 754 until 1870, a period of more than 1100 years.

The emperor, in faraway Constantinople, was indignant when he heard of Pepin's *Donation*. Although he had been powerless to protect Rome and had urged Pope Stephen to appeal to Pepin for aid, he did not wish to lose his control over central Italy. Pepin, however, had no desire to be of service to an emperor who lived hundreds of miles away and who was so weak he could not defend his own possessions. The king had marched against the Lombards only because he was a good Christian and wished to be of service to the Holy Father. So, although the emperor raged and fumed, it did him no good. The people of Rome were delighted with the developments. For several centuries the Pope had been their unofficial ruler and protector. Now he had the title as well as the responsibility. The ties with the old empire were broken forever.

The career of the Papal States was a stormy one from the beginning. Pepin had scarcely recrossed the Alps when Aistulf renounced his promises and marched on Rome. Pope Stephen sent a messenger to Pepin by sea to appeal for help. In his new capacity as protector of the Pope's provinces, Pepin once again marched against the Lombards and defeated them decisively.

Pepin was succeeded as King of the Franks by his son Charlemagne, or Charles the Great. During his reign, the Lombards once again marched on Rome, led by their new king, Desiderius. Answering the appeal of Pope Adrian I, Charlemagne marched across the Alps, defeated the Lombards, and went on to Rome for the Holy Week services. There he renewed the *Donation* of Pepin and added several more cities and the island of Corsica to the Pope's domain. On his way back through Italy he took for himself the title King of the Lombards.

When Pope Leo III was selected in 795 there was a faction

in Rome that was bitterly hostile to him and unjustly accused him of many crimes. The members of this faction were not content with mere accusations. They attacked the Pope and attempted to gouge out his eyes and tear out his tongue. In this they were unsuccessful, but they did wound him grievously. The Pontiff escaped and fled to the court of Charlemagne. That monarch immediately dispatched an army to accompany Leo back to Rome.

Upon being restored to power the Pope insisted that a trial be held and that the accusations against him be heard. Charlemagne considered this event of so much importance that he traveled to Rome in order to be present. The members of the court said that it was not in their power to judge the Pope, and Charlemagne agreed. Therefore the Pope declared on oath that he was innocent of the charges made against him. The men who had attacked him were sentenced to death, but Leo generously changed this to exile.

All this happened just before Christmas in the year 800. On Christmas day while Charlemagne was attending Mass in the Basilica, the Pope suddenly placed a gold crown on his head and a purple cloak across his shoulders. The king was taken entirely by surprise, and did not know the meaning of the action until he heard the choir chanting, "Long life and victory to Charles, the most pious Augustus, crowned by God, the great and pacific Emperor of the Romans." The people in the church thundered their acclaim.

This action of the Pope's was to have a profound influence on the history of Europe for many centuries to come. Charlemagne had been a king; now he was an emperor. The act did not add any new territory to Charlemagne's domain. He was already the ruler of all central Europe including what was later to become France, Germany, Switzerland, Austria, Holland, and Belgium, and parts of what were to become Hungary, Yugoslavia, Rumania, Poland, and Italy. He could have called himself an emperor if he had desired. The action of the Pope, however, signified, that the Church and the Empire were to work together. The Pope was to crown each new emperor, and the emperor was to uphold and protect the Church.

It seemed to be an ideal arrangement. The emperor was to protect the Church and the Papal States. That they needed such protection had been shown by the developments of recent years when the Pope had been beset by the Lombards outside of Rome and by factions opposed to him within the city. Powerful Roman nobles were constantly trying to influence the elections of Popes and each new emperor was to promise, among other things, to guarantee free Papal elections.

The plan seemed perfect from other standpoints also. Most of Europe was to be united under a wise Christian emperor, for the Pope was not to crown any other type. This would mean an end to war and to petty bickerings. The Empire was, in a way, the successor of the old Roman Empire of the West, but whereas the old Empire had been pagan almost to the time of its dissolution, the new one was to be entirely Christian. Its high ideals were shown in the title that was later selected for it, the Holy Roman Empire.

Things did not work out as well as planned, however. When the Saracens invaded the Vatican just 46 years after the crowning of Charlemagne, there was trouble within the Empire, and Pope Leo IV had to gather an army and defeat the invaders with no help from the emperor. It was also with no help from the emperor that he built the famous Leonine Wall around the Vatican.

Later, France separated from the Empire, and the Holy Roman Empire consisted of little more than Germany. The German emperors did not always live up to the promises they had made to protect the Church and the Papal States. Instead of guaranteeing the freedom of Papal elections they often interfered and tried to secure the election of their favorites. Instead of protecting the Papal States from invasion they themselves often invaded Rome.

The story of the struggles between the Popes and the emperors is too long to tell here, but a few incidents may be mentioned. The story of Emperor Henry IV, who made war on the Pope, then crossed the Alps in the dead of winter to beg the Pope's forgiveness, and then resumed the war is related in another chapter.

Frederick Barbarossa was crowned emperor by the only English Pope, Adrian IV. While the emperor and his troops were in Rome for the coronation, trouble broke out and the Germans laid waste the city. The Christian soldiers of a supposedly Christian emperor, who had come to Rome on a peaceful mission, caused more damage in the twelfth century than had the Saracens in the ninth. Then an unexpected ally, malarial fever, came to the Pope's rescue. Barbarossa's soldiers died like flies, and the emperor retreated in haste.

This did not end Barbarossa's threat. He invaded Italy four times, and one time his soldiers marched into St. Peter's itself. The Pope's faithful soldiers fought valiantly till the last, and their blood ran in rivulets over the tomb of St. Peter. The emperor's seeming triumph did not last. In the end, all his enemies united against him, and he was driven out of Italy.

In 1527 came the infamous Sack of Rome. The Spanish and German troops of Emperor Charles V invaded Rome and held it for eight days, killing, burning, and looting. The Pope himself was escorted to safety by his Swiss guards and escaped from Rome.

During these centuries not all the troubles of the Papal States came from the emperors. There were various factions of nobles in Rome who were constantly trying to influence the Papal elections and to seize the temporal power of the Pope. It was largely because of these nobles that the Popes left Rome and resided in Avignon from 1309 to about 1377. The King of France became the protector of the Pope during this period, but he, too, tried to influence the Pope's policies. Protection all too often meant interference. There were also threats from the Saracens, the Turks, the Normans, and other sources too numerous to mention.

Napoleon Bonaparte must be added to the long list of rulers who invaded Rome and seized the temporal power of the Pope. He imprisoned Pope Pius VII and declared himself Emperor of Rome. After his defeat the States of the Church were restored.

So, we see that the history of the Papal States was anything but a peaceful one. Trouble started almost as soon as the *Donation* of Pepin had been made, and it continued for 1100 years. Many times the Pope was imprisoned or forced to flee while an armed conqueror sat on the throne of Rome. All such interruptions to the Pope's power, however, were temporary. It was not until 1870 that the States of the Church came to a definite and permanent end.

King Victor Emmanuel II, of the Italian state of Piedmont, had embarked on a plan of uniting all of Italy under his rule. His chief advisers were Cavour and Garibaldi. In 1860 Victor Emmanuel's troops overran most of the Papal States. The Pope's troops fought bravely but were greatly outnumbered. Four fifths of the Pope's territory was seized and Pope Pius IX was left with little more than the city of Rome.

In 1861 Victor Emmanuel was proclaimed King of Italy, but his supporters were not satisfied. He was a king without a capital, they said, for Rome could be the only true capital of Italy. Twice, toward the end of 1867, the armies of Victor Emmanuel marched toward Rome, but both times they were defeated by a French army which was protecting the Eternal City. In 1870 France became embroiled in a war with Prussia and had to withdraw her army from Rome. This was the oppor-

tunity for which Victor Emmanuel had been waiting. An army
of 60,000 men invaded the territory at three points. The small
company of Papal Zouaves, volunteers from all nations, fought
bravely but were so greatly outnumbered that they could not
stem the tide. They fell back over the open country to make
their final stand in the city of Rome.

On the morning of September 19, the army of Victor
Emmanuel stood before the ancient walls of Rome and demanded
that Pope Pius IX surrender. Pope Pius answered, "Though
we may not prove strong enough to keep the invader from
our homes, we will see that he shall never enter without our
consent. If he persists in acting the part of the robber, we must
treat him as such; if he will use violence and overpower us in
our honest efforts to defend our property, our altars, and our
firesides, let him do so in his true character. Let all right-
minded men have an opportunity to judge him and pronounce
sentence."

That evening the aged Pontiff crossed the piazza to the
Scala Santa and climbed the 27 steps on his knees. Falling
prostrate before the altar he prayed, "If there must be a victim,
O then dear Lord, take me, but spare them. Sacrifice Thy
unworthy servant, Thy undeserving representative. I am old,
too long have I lived; let me be sacrificed. Mercy, O my God,
mercy. But come what may, let Thy Holy Will be done."

As he left the chapel with his attendants, he stopped and
looked down at the tents of the invading army. They stretched
as far as he could see. He looked directly into the mouths of
the enemy cannons. Turning to his own small force in the
Lateran Square he sighed, "Alas they are so very few, but they
are too many to be slaughtered. God's Will be done!"

As he passed the Zouaves on his way to the carriage, they
fell to their knees. After they had received his blessing, they
rose and shouted, "Long live Pius the Ninth, our Pontiff
and our King."

The majestic dome of St. Peter's as seen from the roof of the Basilica.

Two of the great statues atop St. Peter's.

The ancient statue of St. Peter.

The Vatican Buildings from the Piazza of St. Peter's.

International
The stove in which papal ballots are burned.

Press Assn.
White Smoke over the Vatican.

Nuns at work in the Vatican kitchen.

Ballot at papal election cast in gold cup.

The Sistine Chapel where papal elections take place.

The Canopy which remains in place announces to the College of Cardinal
the election of the new pope.

It was dark when the Pope reached the Vatican. He probably knew that he was entering it for the last time, that he should never leave it as long as he lived.

At 5 a.m. the early morning silence was shattered by the roaring of cannons. The assault had started. The old walls held firmly and the Zouaves fought valiantly. Finally the enemy managed to make a break in the wall. The Papal defenders rushed to the breach and met the attackers with a hail of fire. Victor Emanuel's soldiers stopped momentarily. The defense was much greater than they had expected. The Zouaves fixed their bayonets, ready to fight it out hand to hand.

At that moment a white flag arrived. The Pope had ordered his army to surrender. He could not bear to see his soldiers sacrificing their lives in a hopeless cause. The Zouaves were bitterly disappointed. They wished to fight to the end. Many of them wept. It was 10:30 a.m. The battle had lasted five and a half hours. The Papal army had 16 killed and 58 wounded. No one knows how many of the Italian soldiers were killed, but the hospitals of Rome were filled with the wounded.

The flag of the United Kingdom of Italy now flew over Rome. The temporal power of the Pope was gone. The government offered the Pope a large yearly pension, but he refused to accept it. The Papal territory had been stolen from the Church, he said, and if he accepted money he would be in the position of approving the theft. A usurper sat on the throne of Rome, he declared, and in protest, he refused to set foot outside the Vatican. His successors followed his example and remained voluntary prisoners of the Vatican for sixty years.

Many of the supporters of Victor Emmanuel were anti-Catholic. They had hoped that when the temporal power of the Pope came to an end, the Papacy itself would gradually come to an end. In this, they were doomed to bitter disappointment. Catholics the world over sent messages of deep sympathy to the Holy Father. Not only Catholics, but millions of non-Catholics as well, felt that a great injustice had been done. The heart of the Christian world went out to the prisoner of the Vatican.

The Italian government felt the disapproval of the world and squirmed uncomfortably under it. For fifty-nine years "The Roman Question" was one of the most vexing problems facing the government of Italy.

Chapter XIV

THE "PRISONER" IS RELEASED

IN 1870 after the flag of Italy was raised over the city of Rome, the great bronze doors of the Vatican Palace were rolled tightly shut. They remained closed for fifty-nine years in protest against the great injustice that had been done to the Church. During these years five Popes sat on the throne of St. Peter, and not one set foot outside the Vatican grounds. They were called "Prisoners of the Vatican."

Pope Pius IX lived for eight years after his domain had been taken from him. One month before his death he removed the sentence of excommunication from the man who had dethroned him. King Victor Emmanuel on his deathbed was granted permission to receive the Last Sacraments. The Holy Father died February 7, 1878, and even after death he failed to find relief from persecution. His funeral procession was attacked, and his enemies almost succeeded in their attempt to throw his body into the Tiber.

Pope Leo XIII, one of the greatest Pontiffs of all time, succeeded Pope Pius IX. He was so widely respected that he was asked to arbitrate disputes even between non-Catholic powers. Every word he uttered commanded the respect of the world. In a day when the workingman had very few champions indeed, his famous encyclical *Rerum Novarum* earned him the title "Pope of the Workingman." Pope Leo XIII may have been a "prisoner," but he was a prisoner who was admired and respected by the entire world. The government of Italy was finding its position as "jailer" increasingly embarrassing.

Pope Leo XIII was followed by Pope Pius X and he, in turn, was followed by Pope Benedict XV, during whose reign the first World War was fought. Attempts were made to settle the "Roman Question" during the reign of both these pontiffs, but all such attempts ended in failure. Finally, in 1929, during the reign of Pope Pius XI, the successor of Benedict XV, an agreement was reached.

On February 7, 1929, Cardinal Gasparri, Papal Secretary of State, announced to the Vatican Court that a treaty had been made by the Vatican and the Italian government and would be signed February 11 at the Lateran Palace. Shortly afterward the Italian government made the same announcement to its diplomatic corps.

It was raining hard on February 11 when several automobiles containing Cardinal Gasparri and his party drove up to the Lateran Palace. At noon the bells sounded as Premier Mussolini, representing the King of Italy, entered the Hall of Constantine and was met by the Pope's representatives. Only a very few high dignitaries of Church and State were present as Cardinal Gasparri and Premier Mussolini signed the three documents comprising the agreement.

As the signatures were affixed, the bells of St. John Lateran, Mother Church of Christendom, pealed joyously. A group of theological students in the square chanted the *Te Deum*. Cardinal Gasparri presented to Mussolini the gold pen which the Holy Father had sent for the signing. They shook hands and congratulated one another. Then the principals of the great drama left as quietly as they had come. In the driveway, Mussolini's car pulled over to let the Cardinal's pass. The whole history-making event had taken place in less than half an hour. Because the treaty was signed at the Lateran Palace it is known as the Lateran Treaty.

It granted the Holy Father absolute sovereignty over St. Peter's Basilica, the Vatican Palace, and the other buildings of the Vatican. Thus a "brand new" country was created, the tiniest in the world. Vatican City is 108 acres in area, about twice the size of the Capitol grounds in Washington.

This is a far cry from the old Papal States which at one time comprised more than half the Italian peninsula and several islands. This, however, was all the territory the Holy Father desired. The Italian government had offered him more, but he had declined it saying, "I do not desire subjects." The Holy Father did not wish to rule a large number of people. His chief reason for seeking a restoration of temporal power was to secure freedom of action. The Vicar of Christ should not be subject to earthly rulers who might try to influence his actions to suit their selfish purposes.

Pope Pius XI also said that his country was in reality "the largest in the world for it includes the colonnade of Bernini, the dome of Michelangelo, the treasures of science in the gardens and library, the treasures of art in the museums and galleries, and, above all, the tomb of the Prince of the Apostles."

In addition to the Vatican, the Pope became the temporal ruler of fourteen other pieces of territory, including the Concelleria Palace, about a mile from the Vatican in the heart of Rome; the Lateran Palace and the Basilica of St. John Lateran on the eastern edge of Rome; and Castel Gandolfo, a country estate 17 miles southeast of Rome in the Alban hills overlooking Lake Albano. This estate is now the summer home of the Popes.

Besides establishing the temporal power of the Pope, the Lateran Treaty contained several other provisions:

1. The Holy Father surrendered his claim to Rome as well as the remainder of the former Papal States. (Since 1870 the Popes had never ceased to claim possession of this territory.)

2. The Italian government promised to pay an indemnity of $87,500,000 to the Vatican for church property seized in 1870.

3. Italian civil laws which were in conflict with canon law were to be changed so that the two would be in harmony. (Canon law is the name given to all Church laws which relate to faith, morals, and discipline.)

4. Catholicism became the state religion of Italy, and religious instruction was established in the schools.

5. Catholic Action was to be recognized and protected.

Although numerous difficulties afterward arose between the Church and Premier Mussolini, it seemed that after 59 years the "Roman Question" was settled. The actual signing took a very short time, but months of negotiations had preceded it.

Those persons fortunate enough to be in Rome on February 11, 1929, will never forget that great day. All Rome, it seemed, hastened to St. Peter's. More than 70,000 persons of all ranks from laborer to nobleman filled the vast Basilica, and 200,000 more waited in the Square, undaunted by the rain.

At length, silver trumpets sounded, and the Holy Father was borne into the Basilica on a portable throne. He was robed in white and wore his triple crown. Cardinals, bishops, abbots, members of the Papal court, and Vatican guards were in the procession. The choir sang joyously. After Mass the Pontiff yielded to the demands of the crowd outside and appeared on the balcony of St. Peter's to give his blessing to the rain-drenched, cheering throng.

Although the treaty was signed February 11, it did not go into effect until noon on June 7. At that time the government of the new state began to function. Guards from the Vatican Palace took posts at the new boundaries of Vatican City. The bronze doors of the Palace, which had been closed in September, 1870, were rolled back by the Swiss guards. Vatican City took its place among the nations of the world.

At dawn on December 20, 1929, the fiftieth anniversary of his ordination to the priesthood, Pope Pius XI, accompanied by a few attendants, drove in an automobile through the Vatican gate and across Rome to the Church of St. John Lateran, his cathedral church. Only one altar boy served the Pope's low Mass. After Mass the Holy Father mounted his throne and imparted his blessing to those present. Afterward he drove back to his realm, and few people in Rome were aware that the history-making trip had taken place.

Why history making?

It was not the first time Pope Pius XI had left the Vatican. A few months before, he had appeared in St. Peter's Square for the celebration of St. James Day. The trip to the Basilica of St. John Lateran was, however, the first time the Pope had driven across the city of Rome and the first time he had visited his cathedral church. The "Roman Question" had been settled and the Pope was now free to come and go as he chose.

The "Prisoner of the Vatican" was a prisoner no longer.

Chapter XV

MUSSOLINI AND THE POPE

AMERICANS ALWAYS looked with great disapproval upon Benito Mussolini and the Fascist government which he had established in Italy. They did not like the methods he used in rising to power; they liked even less the policies he followed after assuming power. All opposition was ruthlessly crushed. Freedom of the press and freedom of speech were abolished. Italian prisons were filled with persons whose only crime was that they had dared to voice disapproval of certain government policies. Americans, who regard their freedom as their most cherished possession, were greatly shocked by such actions.

Then, in 1929, when the Fascist regime was only six years old, the signing of the Lateran Treaty was announced. The Holy See and the government of Benito Mussolini had reached an agreement which settled the fifty-nine-year-old "Roman Question." Not only did Mussolini grant freedom to the Vatican, but he also agreed to a number of other provisions which seemed of great benefit to the Church.

Persons in America who were unfriendly to the Church were quick to seize upon this. Knowing how most Americans felt toward Mussolini and his Fascist government, they cried, "See, the Catholic Church and Fascism are in perfect agreement! The Church is the enemy of liberty!"

Nothing, of course, could have been farther from the truth. The Church and Fascism were irreconcilably opposed. Fascism said that the State is supreme and that everything else is secondary. The Church says that God comes first and that the heads of the State are accountable to Him. Between these two schools of thought there can be no compromise.

In 1929, for reasons best known to himself, Mussolini desired to reach an agreement with the Holy See. Some authorities said that his popularity with his own people had fallen so low that he sought to restore it and knew of no better way than the settling of the "Roman Question." He restored a small fraction of the land that had been stolen from the Church fifty-nine years before and agreed to a number of other provisions that were no more than just. Pope Pius XI was, naturally, pleased to take what was rightfully his. This in no way meant that he approved of Mussolini's government. He had had many struggles with Mussolini before; he was to have many more in the future. At the time, however, he was glad to reach even a temporary agreement.

❉   ❉   ❉

In the days following World War I conditions in Italy were very bad. Most of the farm land was controlled by wealthy landowners, and the peasants were little more than slaves. In the cities thousands of persons were out of work and did not know where their next meal was coming from. Everyone was discontented. For a while it looked as if Communism might sweep the country.

In 1919 the Catholic Party was formed. It was the purpose of this party to bring about reform by peaceful means. It was so popular that in the same year it was formed it carried 98 of the 508 seats in the Chamber of Deputies and became the second largest political party in Italy.

At the same time Benito Mussolini, a journalist of Milan, was organizing another party, the *Fascisti*. Taking advantage of the chaotic conditions in Italy he advocated immediate reforms. But, in contrast to the Catholic Party, he advocated the use of force. In 1920 Mussolini and a few of his followers managed to get themselves elected to the Chamber of Deputies. This was accomplished largely by means of violence and by intimidating the voters. In the same year the Catholic Party increased its representation to 107.

For two years the battle raged between the two parties. The Catholic Party stood for orderly, democratic reform. The Fascists stood for violence and tyranny. Squads of armed Fascists stormed Catholic schools and churches and the headquarters of the Catholic Party. Despite this the Catholic Party continued to grow and by 1922 had become the largest party in Italy.

Mussolini decided that the time had come to take drastic action. In October, 1922, Fascist militia took over many cities in the northern part of the country and 50,000 militiamen took part in the famous March on Rome. The king, wishing to avoid bloodshed, summoned Mussolini to Rome to form a cabinet. The cabinet contained only four Fascists and eleven members of other parties, but it marked Mussolini's ascent to power.

In the 1923 election the Fascists threw their entire militia into service. They stationed armed men at all polling places. By intimidation and terrorism they managed to gain a majority in the Chamber of Deputies. From that time on, Mussolini had everything his own way. It was not long until he outlawed every party but his own. It became a crime to speak against the Fascists.

Thus Mussolini and his Fascists climbed to power over the murdered corpse of the Catholic Party. If elections had remained free, it is extremely improbable that Mussolini's followers could ever have obtained a majority. But force and terrorism won. Democracy was crushed.

Those who say that a friendly alliance existed between the Catholic Church and Fascism forget that it was the Catholic Party that was Mussolini's strongest opposition before he seized the reins of power. Mussolini always considered the Catholics as his enemies, but he was never able to crush them completely. Italy is ninety per cent Catholic, and there are limits even to the power of a ruthless dictator. It was not by accident that there was never a single Catholic among the leaders of Fascism.

For a while there was peace between Catholicism and Fascism. Mussolini seemed bent upon winning the good will of the Catholics. He restored religious teaching in the schools. He banned immoral publications. He put crucifixes everywhere, even in the Colosseum. These actions did not mislead the Pope or any other intelligent Catholic, who knew that beneath this show of friendliness the old hostility still smoldered.

In 1926 Fascism showed itself in its true colors when it established the Balilla and the Avanguardisti. All boys in Italy from eight to fourteen were forced to join the former, those from fourteen to eighteen the latter. By the time they were eighteen they had to go into the army. The boys in the two organizations wore uniforms and received a military education. They were constantly taught that their greatest duty was to Italy, that they must give their minds, their hearts, and their bodies to their country. In democratic countries these boys would have been happy, carefree school children. In Italy they were in uniform being trained as soldiers.

Organizations somewhat similar to the Balilla and the Avanguardisti were started for the girls. They were called the Little Italians (Piccole Italiane) and the Young Italians (Giovani Italiane). The members of these groups also wore uniforms and received military training.

It is only too easy to see the purpose of these organizations. The Fascists took the children when they were eight years old and undertook to train them for the remainder of their lives. Children brought up in this manner knew nothing but Fascism and became fanatics in their devotion to the party and the State.

Fascism could tolerate no competition in the field of training the youth. For years the Catholic Boy Scouts had furnished boys with wholesome recreation and with moral and religious training. On January 9, 1927, Mussolini abolished all Catholic Boy Scouts in towns of less than 20,000 population. The remaining Scouts were forced to carry the Fascist emblem on their banners.

Pope Pius XI had already protested against the formation of the Balilla. Now he was forced to accede to the dissolution of a large part of the Catholic Boy Scouts. In doing so he called the Scouts "the apple of my eye" and made it clear that he was giving way to force alone.

The Fascists were not content with this victory. On March 30 they ordered the suppression of all Catholic Boy Scouts. Again, the Vatican had to bow to superior force.

Catholic Action was an organization which had been founded by Pope Pius XI and which was very dear to his heart. This organization also incurred the wrath of the Fascists because it was not under their control. Whatever they could not control they were determined to destroy. In 1924 Fascist mobs attacked two hundred headquarters of Catholic Action scattered throughout Italy. The Pope immediately sent 500,000 lire to the president of the organization for the purpose of repairing part of the damage. In 1925 and in 1926 there was violence against Catholics in Florence and Pisa. The men who had wreaked the damage in Pisa were brought to trial but were not convicted, for no judge dared to sentence a Fascist.

The situation was so serious in August, 1926, that the Holy Father called off the international gymnastic tournament of the Catholic Federation of Europe which had been scheduled to take place in Rome early in September.

The control which the state exercised over the workingman was another cause of friction. The Church, since the time of Leo XIII, had encouraged the formation of labor unions and had fostered friendly relations between employers and employees. Fascism insisted on a rigid control over labor, just as it did over everything else. Workers were no longer free to strike or to bargain collectively. They became little more than slaves. The Church disapproved heartily but was powerless to do anything about the situation.

In the midst of all these struggles came the signing of the Lateran Treaty in February, 1929. Just why Premier Mussolini saw fit to establish peace at that moment is not known. Certain it is that he did not have the welfare of the Church at heart. He was as much an enemy of Catholicism as ever.

While Americans who were hostile to the Church were crying that there was an alliance between the Church and Fascism, Mussolini was giving the lie to their statements by resuming his attacks. In May, 1929, when the signatures on the Lateran Treaty were scarcely dry, he made a speech in which he said that the Church in Italy was not free and that Vatican City was a "protectorate" of the Kingdom of Italy.

"We have buried the temporal power of the Pope, not resuscitated it," he said.

In describing the rise of Christianity he said: "This religion was born in Palestine but became Catholic in Rome. If it had been confined to Palestine, it would in all probability never have been more than one of the numerous sects which flourished in that overheated environment. . . . The chances are that it would have perished and left no trace."

In making this statement the Duce showed himself not only shockingly irreverent but also appallingly ignorant of history. When the Popes left Rome for Avignon, the city suffered more than the Church. Grass grew in its streets and wolves prowled through what had once been populous sections of the city.

About education Mussolini said, "In this field I am intractable. Education must be ours. Our children must be educated in our religious faith, but we must round out this education, and we must give our youths a sense of virility and the power of conquest."

Pope Pius XI replied the next day in the famous speech in which he referred to Mussolini as the devil. He attacked the idea that education should be entirely in the hands of the State, and said that the State should not teach children to become conquerors. "What would happen if all the other states educated their people for conquest?

"We can never agree with anything," he said, "which restricts or denies the right which nature and God gave the Church and the family in the field of education. On this point we are not merely intractable, but we are uncompromising."

Then came the famous statement: "When it is a question of saving a few souls and impeding the accomplishment of greater damage to souls, we feel courage to treat with the devil in person. And it was exactly with the purpose of preventing greater evil that we negotiated with the devil some time ago when the fate of our dear Catholic Boy Scouts was decided."

Catholic Action continued to flourish during the next year or two. The Fascists watched this with growing resentment. Their newspapers declared that Catholic Action was preparing to seize power. "It is time to take extreme measures," said one of the papers.

Throughout Italy, Fascist mobs attacked everything Catholic. In one city two priests were assaulted. In others, headquarters of Catholic Action were plundered. Bombs were thrown. Statues of the saints were smashed. In one city Fascists marched through the streets with an oil painting of the Pope and finally trampled it with cries of "Traitor!" A bishop's house was set on fire. The Catholics called the police, but every time the police arrived just too late.

Most of these facts were hidden from the world at large, for the Fascists clamped down a strict censorship. The Vatican newspaper *Osservatore Romano* was the only publication that told of the outrages, and the Italian police seized most of the copies of it.

On June 29, 1931, however, the world was made aware in a dramatic fashion of the persecution that the Church was undergoing in Italy. The Pope had written a long encyclical stating the facts in detail. He knew that if the Fascists could possibly prevent the publishing of the encyclical they would most certainly do so. Therefore he called in Monsignor Francis J. Spellman, now Archbishop of New York, and Monsignor Vanneufville, a prominent French clergyman, and asked them to take the encyclical to France. The two priests flew to France with the encyclical, and there it was released to the world on June 29.

Everyone was struck by the fact that it was necessary to take the encyclical out of Italy before its contents could be released. Non-Catholics as well as Catholics read the message with the greatest sympathy.

"They have tried," said the Pope in the encyclical, "to strike to death all that was and will be always dearest to our heart." He spoke of numerous "brutalities and beatings, blows and bloodshed," and mentioned the fact that authorities always seemed to approve of this violence against the Church.

He deplored the educational program which monopolized completely "the young from their tenderest years up to manhood and womanhood, for the exclusive advantage of a party and of a regime based on an ideology that clearly resolves itself into a true, a real pagan worship of the State. . . .

"A conception of the State which makes the young generation belong entirely to it, without any exception, from the tenderest years up to adult life, cannot be reconciled by a Catholic with the Catholic doctrine and cannot, either, be reconciled with the natural right of the family."

Fascism, said the Holy Father, encouraged the people under its control "to indulge in insulting words and actions against the father of the faithful, even to cry out 'Down with the Pope and death to him!' . . . " This "cannot in any way be reconciled with Catholic doctrine and practice."

He condemned all those who persecuted Catholic Action "which, as is universally known, the Church and its head regard as very dear and precious."

He then took up the matter of the oath which the Fascists forced all Italians, even little children, to take. The oath was: "I swear to obey the orders of the Duce without questioning them and to serve the cause of the Fascist Revolution with all my force and if necessary with my blood." Such an oath is, of course, contrary to all Catholic teachings, for no human being can set himself above the laws of God. The Holy Father said in no uncertain terms, "Such an oath as it stands is unlawful."

Pope Pius realized, however, that since the Fascists were in complete control of Italy many persons were forced to take the oath against their wills. "We have sought to find a way which would restore tranquillity to these consciences, reducing to a minimum the external difficulties of the situation. It seems to us that such a means for those who have already received the membership card would be to make for themselves before God, in their own consciences, a reservation such as 'saving the laws of God and of the Church,' or 'in accordance with the duties of a good Christian,' with the firm proposal to declare also externally such a reservation if the need of it arose."

All this just two years after the signing of the Lateran Treaty!

On February 12, 1932, the third anniversary of the signing of the treaty, Mussolini was received in solemn audience by the Holy Father. Once more the dictator had decided to make peace with the Church. He later paid a visit to the Basilica where he and his attendants knelt down to pray before the tomb of St. Peter. This marked the beginning of three years of fairly satisfactory relations between Church and State.

In 1936 Mussolini concluded an alliance with Adolf Hitler, dictator of Germany, an alliance of which the Pontiff could not approve. Bad as Fascism had been up to that time, Hitler's Nazism was infinitely worse. Hitler was even more ruthless than Mussolini in his persecution of all those who differed with him. When Italy followed Germany's lead in persecuting the Jews, the Pope protested vigorously.

In 1938 Hitler was planning to visit Rome and the streets of that city were decked in swastikas in anticipation of the coming event. The Holy Father said that he deeply regretted to see in Rome a cross that was "not the Cross of Christ." He very pointedly left Rome and went to his summer home at Castel Gandolfo while Hitler was in the city.

Mussolini paid no attention to the very evident displeasure of the Holy Father. He was bent upon world conquest and was sure that his alliance with Nazi Germany was the surest way of achieving that conquest.

In 1938 when Germany and Italy were threatening the peace of the world, Pope Pius XI begged God to take his life and to avert the terrible war which seemed so imminent. As if in answer to this request, the saintly Pontiff died a few months later, and the Munich Conference granted the world one more year of peace.

When Premier Mussolini came back from the Munich conference, he was cheered wildly by his people. Those in a position to observe Mussolini said that he seemed greatly disappointed. For fifteen years he had been educating his people for war and conquest, and now he had reached the height of his popularity because his people thought he had succeeded in preventing war! In another year and a half Mussolini was to launch his treacherous attack upon defeated France and so plunge his peace-loving people into the war. At the time of the Munich Conference, however, they did not know this. He was never to be so popular again.

Pope Pius XII, who ascended the throne of St. Peter in March, 1939, took up the work of his predecessor and worked feverishly to prevent the outbreak of war. A few months later the Germans invaded Poland and France, and Great Britain declared war on Germany. The Pope then devoted his efforts to preventing the spread of the war. In this he seemed to have the coöperation of Mussolini who surprised everyone by remaining neutral for some time after his Axis partner had gone to war.

"But," says Camille M. Cianfarra, who was Vatican correspondent for the New York *Times* at the time, "while the Pope's policy was dictated by humanitarian motives — the prevention of bloodshed and destruction — Mussolini's policy was merely the result of what he thought to be a shrewd calculation. Italy's dictator was gaining time, while preparing to enter the war in its last stages, that is, when Hitler had disposed of France for him. He played a hypocritical game with the Pope, encouraging the hope that Italy really intended to remain neutral."

In June, 1940, when France was on the verge of collapse, Mussolini decided that his moment had come and he declared war upon France. He was sure that the collapse of Great Britain would follow almost immediately, and that he would find himself on the winning side of the war without having to do very much fighting. Subsequent events have proved him to be one of the worst guessers in history, but his bad guess was to bring untold sufferings upon his own people as well as those of other nations.

Immediately upon Italy's entrance into the war, says Mr. Cianfarra, Mussolini's policy in regard to the Vatican underwent a drastic change. "The Pontiff was made to understand that Italy would tolerate no interference on the part of the Vatican. . . . Priests throughout the country were told by local Fascist officials that the preaching of peace and brotherhood among men, in keeping with the tenets of the Catholic faith, was in conflict with the Fascist doctrine and Italy's war effort. Those who opposed Mussolini's policy of 'hatred' for the English were warned and, in many cases, arrested and sent to concentration camps or jails."

The semiofficial Vatican newspaper *Osservatore Romano* was the only paper in all Italy giving real news. At the outbreak of the war the circulation of this publication jumped from 30,000 to 100,000. In 1939 young Fascists began beating delivery men in the streets. Priests found reading the paper were also beaten. At the beginning of 1940, sale on the streets was prohibited. When Italy entered the war in June, 1940, the mailing of *Osservatore Romano* was halted for three months.

At that time an announcement appeared in *Osservatore Romano* stating that the paper would cease publication. This apparently frightened the Fascists, for beatings in the streets stopped and deliveries came through. The paper never actually ceased publication but for a while it confined itself to religious news.

Recent Popes have been outspoken in their denunciation of Russian Communism, for the Russian government had announced its intention to abolish religion. It was the only government in the world that had officially adopted atheism. Therefore when Germany and Italy launched their attack upon Russia in June, 1940, they announced it as a crusade of the Christian world against Godless Bolshevism, and they hoped that Pope Pius XII would bless their cause. If he had, the moral advantage to their side would have been great.

The Pontiff, however, was too wise to fall into this trap. He knew that the attack on Russia was part of the war for world conquest and not a religious crusade. Instead of endorsing the war, he maintained a complete silence regarding it. As the months went by, Mussolini became more and more irritated by this attitude, but the Pope did not waver.

During the war the popularity of the Pope reached a new high with the peace-loving Italian people. They had already

had five years of fighting in Ethiopia and Spain and were sick
of it. When Mussolini dragged them into a new war, they felt
they had been betrayed. This opinion was confirmed when
German soldiers and secret police filtered into Italy and that
country became a mere vassal of Germany. Meanwhile casu-
alties were mounting and food and other necessities were becoming scarce.

The people knew that Pope Pius XII had done everything in
his power to prevent the war and to prevent Italy's entering it.
They gave him great ovations wherever he went. Thousands of
persons attended his audiences. A little paper called *La Paralo
del Papa* (the Word of the Pope), which published nothing but
the Pope's speeches, attained a huge circulation. In spite of everything Mussolini had been able to do, the Church was still very
much in the hearts of the people while Mussolini himself was
detested by them. He would have been swept out of power if he
had not been supported by foreign soldiers.

The lot of Italy in the war was an unhappy one from the
first, and things became successively worse. Her campaign
against Greece would have ended in complete disaster if the
Germans had not come to the rescue. The great might of the
United States was thrown into the war against her. Her Afri-
can empire was lost. Her fleet was whittled away. Her cities
were bombed. Italian soil was invaded when American, British,
and Canadian troops landed in Sicily and proceeded to fight
their way across the island.

For three and a half years after Italy had entered the war,
Rome was not molested by enemy bombers. The city owed its
privileged position among belligerent capitals to the fact that
the Holy Father lived close by. On July 19, 1943, Rome's
immunity from bombing came to a sudden and nerve-shattering
end when a fleet of American bombers appeared over the city
and dropped their deadly loads on the freight yards. The city
rocked with explosions. The people of Rome, most of whom

had come to think that they would never be bombed, were panic stricken.

The nearest bomb hit to Vatican City was more than a mile away, but Pope Pius XII could see and hear the bombardment. He knelt down and prayed fervently for the people of Rome and of the world. When the bombing was over, he got into his black limousine and rode forth to inspect the damage and to console the people. The terrorized populace greeted him as badly frightened children might greet a kind and protecting father. They crowded about him, begging his blessing and his prayers. "Il Papa," they shouted, "Il Papa!" Several times the Pontiff seemed in danger of being crushed as the people surged about him. Everywhere he went Pope Pius gave his blessing and led the people in prayer. The Fascist leaders that had so loudly and boastfully led the nation into the war were nowhere to be seen.

A few days later came the sensational news that Mussolini had "resigned" as premier of Italy. The world could hardly believe the news at first. For twenty years Mussolini had ruled Italy with an iron hand. People had become so accustomed to seeing his jutting jaw in newspaper pictures and in newsreels and to reading his boastful speeches that they found it difficult to imagine Italy without its bombastic *duce*.

Mussolini's "resignation" and arrest had been ordered by the King at the prompting of the military leaders. These leaders knew that Italy was helpless before the onslaught of the Allies, and they knew that it would be much easier to make peace if Mussolini were out of the way. He was subsequently "rescued" by German parachutists and taken to northern Italy where he was made head of a puppet government. The German leaders, including Hitler, at whose instigation it was set up, did not take this government seriously. Mussolini could not but feel the ignominy of his position. The great dictator, who had once made the world tremble, was now nothing but a stooge for Adolf Hitler, who himself was on the losing end of a war.

The removal of Mussolini did not mean the end of the troubles of Pope Pius XII; for the Nazi seizure of Rome came soon after that, and the Pontiff's troubles were increased a hundredfold. His removal did mean, however, the end of one more powerful enemy of the Church.

The story of Mussolini and the Popes is the same old story all over again. A powerful ruler arises and is so impressed by his own importance that he sets himself above everybody and everything. Because the Pope represents authority also, even though it is authority of a different kind, he is determined that the Pope must be brought under his control. For a while he seems to meet with success. He has great armies behind him. The Pope has nothing behind him — except the word of our Lord that the Church shall endure until the end of time and that the gates of hell shall not prevail against it.

The contest always seems so pitifully one-sided at the beginning. An armed conqueror against an unarmed spiritual leader. But the end is always the same. The conqueror, so successful at first, goes down in inglorious defeat and the Church goes on — as it will till the end of time.

PART V

The Vatican Today

Chapter XVI

MODERNIZING THE VATICAN

AFTER THE signing of the Lateran Treaty, the quiet that had reigned over the Vatican for so many years was suddenly shattered. The clanging of hammers, the buzzing of saws, the constant din of riveting machines broke the stillness. A thousand workmen were assigned to the construction work that was necessary when the Vatican became an independent nation. The government of the new country had to be housed, and communication had to be established with the outside world.

Most of the construction work took place on the slope of the hill behind the Vatican Gardens. This area had not previously been a part of the Vatican but had been given to the Holy Father by the Lateran Treaty. Squalid old houses which had stood on the hill were torn down and the gardens extended. In the midst of the gardens were erected a new railway station, the Governor's Palace, the radio station, and various residences of high officials of the Vatican.

The new Pontifical Railroad Station was built at the expense of the Italian government. It is connected with the Italian state railways by a viaduct of eight arches. The station is an imposing stone structure and contains a marble hall of honor where kings and other distinguished visitors may be received.

The railway system is the shortest in the world, less than one sixth of a mile. It is very important, however, for Vatican City produces none of the things it needs and is wholly dependent upon the outside world.

Not far from the railroad station is the new Governor's Palace. Up until the present time there has been but one governor of Vatican City, Marquis Camillo Serafini. Pope Pius XI delegated his temporal power to Serafini immediately after the signing of the Lateran Treaty, and the present Pontiff has retained him as governor. Besides being the home of the governor, the Palace serves two other purposes. It houses the administrative offices of Vatican City and it contains apartments for the lodging of distinguished guests.

Station HVJ, the "Voice of the Papacy," was erected near the remains of the old wall of Leo IV, built in the ninth century. It was built and presented to Pope Pius XI by Guglielmo Marconi, the inventor of radio. The Holy Father followed very closely the entire installation and discussed every phase of it with Marconi. Daily broadcasts are made from the station in many different languages. Every time the Supreme Pontiff addresses the world by radio it is through Station HVJ.

When Vatican City became a nation, it had to start its own postal system and issue its own postage stamps. This meant enlarging the post office. Today the post office is a profitable institution employing fifteen persons. Before the war it sold about $80,000 worth of stamps a year, most of them to stamp collectors. When Pope Pius XI died and Pope Pius XII was elected, the post office set a new record, selling $60,000 worth of stamps in two months. An average of 60 pounds of letters and cards a day are handled by the post office, and about 100 pounds of printed matter.

The post-office building also houses the new telegraph office which ordinarily handles about eighty telegrams a day. On special days, such as anniversaries, thousands of congratulatory telegrams are received. The first telegram to be sent from the office was a message from Pope Pius XI to the King of Italy when the Lateran Treaty was ratified. Pope Pius XI's forty-thousand-word encyclical on labor was wired from this office. It was wired so that it would reach all parts of the world at the same time.

The new telephone system was the particular joy of Pope Pius XI who watched its installation with great interest. The task of installing it was an extremely delicate one, for wires had to be placed in walls which were covered with priceless murals. The system was the gift of the International Telephone and Telegraph Company.

Vatican City has more telephones in proportion to its population than any other country in the world. There is a phone for nearly every person. There are phones everywhere in the Vatican, from the underground workshops to the dome of St. Peter's. The Holy Father's telephone number is 101, but his phone is never rung without his consent.

Power for the radio station, the telegraph system, and for all the other Vatican needs is supplied by a new central power plant. A new central heating plant is in the same building. No other country in the world has all its buildings heated by one central plant.

A short distance from the Vatican proper and near the Castel Sant'Angelo, a new Papal Palace of Justice was erected. This palace contains a courtroom and a jail with three cells. Both the courtroom and the jail are used rarely, for the residents of Vatican City are law-abiding people. The first prisoner arrested after the creation of Vatican City was a man who had robbed Peter's Pence box in St. Peter's.

Not all the changes brought about in the Vatican under the reign of Pope Pius XI were made necessary by the Lateran Treaty. The new Picture Gallery, for example, would probably have been built even if the treaty had never been signed. This gallery is unique in that it contains no windows. It houses one of the greatest collections of paintings to be found anywhere.

A new entrance was made in the wall on the northern side of the Vatican so that visitors to the new Picture Gallery and the other museums would not have to traverse the whole of Vatican City. Since the museums are higher than the city outside, a great concrete shaft was built with circular ramps for the ascent and descent of automobiles. Pedestrians are accommodated by elevators in the shaft.

Many other changes were brought about in the Vatican during the reign of Pope Pius XI. A new mosaic studio was erected; the Vatican library was enlarged; new barracks were provided for the Swiss guards; a new office was given to *Osservatore Romano,* the daily newspaper published by the Vatican.

Even this list, impressive as it is, does not tell the entire story of the modernization program carried out by Pope Pius XI in his territory. This Pontiff will undoubtedly be remembered as one of the greatest builder Popes of history.

Chapter XVII

THE SMALLEST COUNTRY IN THE WORLD

ALL CENTURIES meet in Vatican City. The museums and the library contain records of civilizations which flourished and died long before Christ walked the earth. The tombs of St. Peter and the other Apostles are reminders of the early years of the infant Church. The wall of Leo IV, a large section of which is still standing, was erected during the ninth century. It would be impossible to find a century that is not represented within the confines of the little state. Yet, it is the spirit of the Middle Ages which seems to dominate the entire atmosphere.

The Papal realm with its broadcasting station, its power plant, its telephone, telegraph, and railroad systems, is completely modern. Yet, in spite of all this, a visitor to Vatican City has the feeling that he has suddenly been transplanted into the Middle Ages.

When the stranger presents himself at the stout iron gate to the right of St. Peter's, he finds several members of the Swiss guards standing sentry. The guards wear uniforms of black, red, and yellow and have helmets of burnished steel. Their weapons are ancient halberds, combination spears and battle axes. This is the same way the guards have dressed for four hundred years. Some of the helmets, in fact, are the very ones that have been worn since the sixteenth century.

After being stopped by the Swiss guards, if the visitor presents the proper credentials, he is admitted to the Vatican grounds. Here the impression of having moved back several centuries is heightened. Deep silence reigns over the almost deserted streets. The noise of the outside traffic is completely cut off.

The buildings have an ancient look. Papal gendarmes move about in pairs, wearing cocked hats and carrying curved swords at their sides. Most of the people seen in the streets are priests, bishops, or cardinals wearing their black cassocks. The visitor might encounter the Pope's secret chamberlains dressed in Elizabethan costume, with stiff starched ruffs around their necks and jeweled rapiers at their waists. The traveler feels that his modern dress strikes a jarring note in this atmosphere of the Middle Ages.

The 1025 inhabitants of Vatican City lead a life that is far removed from that of the city of Rome. Most of them are ecclesiastics. In peacetime the only laymen are 100 Swiss guards, 150 gendarmes, 6 firemen (who also run the Vatican elevators and the telephone exchanges), the governor, some servants, and a few others. After Italy entered the war the diplomats accredited to the Holy See temporarily took up their residence there. The population is almost entirely male.

There is a food shop for the convenience of the inhabitants. Most supplies are cheaper in Vatican City than in Rome because there are no import duties. There is also a drugstore and several other stores. Sale of all merchandise is a government monopoly. No person can run a shop or an office or a studio without the authorization of the governor. This prevents commercializing the most interesting city in the world.

A filling station is provided for the few automobiles that are allowed in Vatican City. The licenses bear the letters S.C.V. (State of the City of the Vatican). The first five numbers belong to the Holy Father and are in red. The other ninety or so are in black. Most of the automobiles bearing a Vatican City license belong to cardinals and other high dignitaries.

The first Vatican automobile was presented to Pope Pius XI

in 1922 by the people of Milan. The Pope was delighted with it. Since there was no provision for automobiles, it had to be kept in the pontifical stables. The car was used by the Holy Father to drive about the Vatican grounds, for at that time he was still a "prisoner."

The residents of Vatican City are early risers, the Holy Father himself setting the example. While most of surrounding Rome sleeps, the priests of Vatican City are saying Mass. Servants set out for Rome to buy some of the supplies that cannot be obtained in the local shops.

At the crack of dawn the gates are opened and Rome street cleaners are admitted. On the day after Vatican City became an independent state, the usual force of street cleaners appeared but was refused admittance by the Swiss guards. They had strict orders not to admit anyone who did not have the proper credentials. As a result, the streets remained uncleaned for several days until the governor's attention was called to the situation. He at once made the necessary arrangements with the governor of Rome, and ever since the street cleaners have been admitted every morning. Vatican City is the only country in the world that has its streets cleaned every day by employees of a foreign country.

About 9 o'clock a stream of people go to work in Vatican City. The offices, library, museums, and gardens require a host of clerks, attendants, servants, ushers, doormen, waiters, gardeners, and many other workers. Most of these people live in Rome.

Throngs of sight-seers flock to the museums during the day, but since the new entrance has been built these people no longer have to cross the rest of Vatican City. Persons seeking an audience with the Pope or having business with Vatican officials are admitted after being questioned by the Swiss guards. Most of these people move about on foot so they do not seriously disturb the traditional calm of the Vatican.

At 4 o'clock the library, museums, and offices close. The visitors and workers go home. The Holy Father usually takes advantage of this quiet period to go to the Vatican gardens for his daily walk.

At nightfall the gates of Vatican City are closed and all activities cease. The streets, except for the gendarmes making their rounds, are deserted. The inhabitants retire early for they have been up since dawn. Another day has ended in the tiny country that is the center of the Christian world.

Chapter XVIII

THE POPE'S ARMY

VATICAN CITY is a very new country, dating only from 1929. It has, however, one of the oldest armies in the world — the Swiss guards. Before Columbus discovered America the Popes had bodyguards of Catholic Swiss. In 1505 Julius II made a treaty with the Swiss cantons of Zurich and Lucerne in which the cantons agreed to furnish a guard of their best soldiers to protect the Holy Father and his palace. Even today the Swiss constitution, which forbids citizens bearing arms for foreign states, makes an exception in the case of the Papal army.

The guards have distinguished themselves for heroism many times. The infamous Sack of Rome took place in May, 1527, when the corps was just 22 years old. Faithful to their trust, the Swiss guards conducted Pope Clement VII to safety in the Castel Sant'Angelo, though nearly all of them lost their lives.

At the start of World War II there were 100 guards. When the guards were organized in 1505, they numbered 250. At one time in the sixteenth century their number was increased to 600. The guards were not disbanded even after the Italian forces had seized the Pope's possessions in 1870. The Holy Father had an army even though he no longer had a country.

The guards are very picturesque in the black, red, and yellow uniforms. The style of these uniforms has never been changed. It is the same as that of the sixteenth century. They are said to have been designed by Michelangelo, although there seems to be some doubt about this. On special occasions the guards wear steel breastplates. On day duty they often carry ancient halberds, combination spears and battle axes; on night duty they carry modern rifles and bayonets. Machine guns are a part of their equipment.

Because of their colorful uniforms, visitors sometimes think that the guards are for decoration only; this is far from true. They are a well-drilled, disciplined military corps. They are under the command of a colonel, a lieutenant colonel, a major, and two captains.

The guards are responsible for protecting the person of the Holy Father and also his possessions. They guard the four entrances to Vatican City and the doors to the Holy Father's apartments. They attend all solemn functions in St. Peter's and the Vatican. In all public processions they have their place. When the Pope is carried on his throne chair, he is surrounded by six Swiss guards carrying large swords.

A guard must be a native Swiss, a Catholic, and physically perfect. He must be at least five feet eight inches in height, and at the time of his enlistment must be between the ages of nineteen and twenty-five and unmarried. He must have been graduated from a school for noncommissioned officers in Switzerland. After a year of good conduct the cost of his journey to Rome is refunded. He may leave the corps at any time if he gives three months' notice. After eighteen years of service he is entitled to a pension for life amounting to half his pay; after twenty-five years to two thirds of his pay; and after thirty years to his full pay.

The guards are on duty for twenty days and then receive ten days' rest. They receive a furlough of three months every three years. They have their own chapel, chaplain, barracks, football team, and trumpet corps. Most of the guards speak German, for they come from the German-speaking section of Switzerland.

The administration of the oath to the new recruits takes place in the Belvedere Court. The guards march into the court and

Swiss
Guard
on
sentry
duty.

Free Lance

view of the Swiss Guard.

The private chapel of the Pope.

International The late Pope Pius XI at his desk.

Pope Pius XII reading his first appeal for peace, after his election.

ambassador about to present his credentials to the Pope.

A shady walk in the Vatican Gardens.

International News

Pope Pius XII as he prayed for the end of the bombing of Rome in August, 19

Before the war visits of prelates and clergy of the Eastern Churches were freque

Main reading room of the Vatican Library.

card
logue of
Vatican
ary
made by
erican
rians.

Palace of the Vatican City Government.

The Vatican Gallery of Paintings.

at a command from their colonel the new recruits step forward. "Do you promise to serve faithfully and loyally for the duration of your service the reigning Pope Pius XII and his legitimate successors?" they are asked. Touching the satin banner of the guards with their left hand and raising their right hand, they answer that they do so promise. Then they sing a hymn. They are now full-fledged members of the Holy Father's bodyguard and ready to lay down their lives if necessary to protect him.

The members of the Swiss guards all belong to good families and are well above the average mentally and physically. In their native Switzerland they could earn much more than the small salary that is paid to them at the Vatican. They have something far more important than money, however. Theirs is the rare privilege of guarding the life and property of the Holy Father, Christ's representative on earth.

The Swiss guards make up the army of Vatican City, and the Papal gendarmes are its police force. The gendarmes number 150 and have five officers. In order to qualify as Papal gendarmes, the men must have completed a period of service in the Italian army and have secured certificates of good character. They must be at least five feet nine inches in height. It is their duty to police the palace and gardens. They have a new barracks which was built during the reign of Pius XI. Like the Swiss guards they have a music corps which gives concerts on special occasions. They are subject to the prefect of apostolic palaces.

Besides the Swiss guards and the Pontifical gendarmes, the Holy Father has two other military groups, the Palatine guards of honor, and the noble guards.

The Palatine guards were established in 1850. Their uniform consists of a high military hat called a shako which falls over the nape of the neck and has a slender red plume in front, dark blue trousers, and tunics trimmed in crimson and gold. They have sword belts, cartridge boxes, and rifle straps all in white with a dagger and a sheath of nickel. They carry old model rifles. Unlike the Swiss guards and the Papal gendarmes, they are not full-time professionals and receive no pay for their services; they are given only an allowance with which to buy their uniforms. Ordinarily their duties consist mainly of standing guard during solemn functions and papal processions.

During the German occupation of Rome, however, these guards were increased in number and called to full-time duty. More than 150 were stationed within the Vatican itself. Smaller detachments were stationed at all buildings which had been placed under the Holy Father's jurisdiction by the Lateran Treaty.

When Vatican City was bombed on November 5, 1943, two of these guards, faithful to their orders, remained at their posts near the spot where the bombs fell. They were later cited for this action in an order of the day issued by the commander of the corps.

The noble guards were originally a cavalry group and served actively. In the time of Leo XIII they still rode alongside the papal coach when the Pope rode in his gardens. Today the guards make their appearance only when the Holy Father takes part in a public function. When the Pope withdraws, he is always followed by the noble guard. It is the privilege of the noble guards to convey to newly created cardinals the tidings of their election. They travel to all parts of the world to do this. Whenever a new cardinal is appointed in the United States, a member of the noble guards comes here to tell him officially of his appointment.

The noble guards belong to the noble families of the old Papal States. They must be between the ages of twenty-one and twenty-five when admitted to the corps, at least five feet seven inches in height, and physically perfect. They must have a testimonial that they are of good character from their parish priest, bishop, or some other ecclesiastical authority. Their commander is appointed by the Supreme Pontiff and is always a Roman prince. Otherwise promotion is regulated exclusively by length of service.

At the present time the noble guards number seventy. They are commanded by a major general. Their uniform consists of a black coat with gold epaulets, dark blue trousers, and a steel helmet with a gold crest. They wear a gold crossbelt with an ornament bearing the letters G.N.P. (*Guardia Nobile Papale*).

It is an honor indeed to belong to any of these groups which guard the Holy Father and the Vatican grounds. It is truly fitting that only the finest men are protectors of the center of Christianity and the Vicar of Christ on earth.

PART VI
A Trip to St. Peter's

Chapter XIX

ACROSS ST. PETER'S SQUARE

ST. PETER'S is the largest and most famous church in the world. Although it is not the Pope's cathedral church, it is the one most commonly associated with him. It is here that he presides at jubilees, canonizations, and all other solemn functions. It is here that the coronation ceremonies take place when he receives the Papal crown. On these occasions more than 80,000 persons assemble in the great halls of St. Peter's. Through newsreels and newspaper pictures, the main altar of the Basilica with its great bronze covering, or baldachin, is a familiar sight to millions of persons who have never visited Rome.

If it were not for St. Peter's, the home of the Pope would not be where it is. As we have already seen, the old St. Peter's was built over the tomb of the Apostle Peter, and the buildings of the Vatican were erected to accommodate visitors to the tomb. It was not until many centuries later that the Popes came to live at the Vatican.

St. Peter's is the first sight every visitor to Rome wishes to see. His first view of the famous church, just after he crosses the River Tiber, is an awe-inspiring one. A wide avenue leads from the river straight to the magnificent square, or Piazza, and behind the square is the Basilica itself. From here the church and square can be seen in all their beauty. The vast expanse of pavement in the Piazza, the fountains, the columns enclosing the square on two sides, the front of the church, and the great dome of Michelangelo are beheld as one great, harmonious, breath-taking whole.

As the visitor approaches the Basilica the dome seems to disappear. According to Michelangelo's plans the dome would have been perfectly visible from the square. When Michelangelo died, however, his successor, Maderna, saw fit to change the plans. He extended the front of the church much farther than Michelangelo had intended. Most lovers of architecture say that this was a serious mistake, for now the great dome, the most magnificent in the world, can be seen only from a distance.

The avenue leading from the Tiber to St. Peter's is a new one; it was completed during the reign of the present Pope, Pius XII. A great number of houses were torn down in order to build it. It is only fitting that the beautiful church, planned by some of the most gifted architects the world has ever known, should have an approach worthy of it.

The new avenue is bordered on one side by the famous covered "passage" which united the Vatican to Castel Sant' Angelo. The passage was built in order to establish a communication between the dwelling of the Popes and the fortress of the city of Rome. It was through this passage that the Swiss guards conducted Pope Clement VII to the safety of the Castel during the Sack of Rome in 1527. Part of the passage was built on a still older landmark, the wall of Leo IV, erected in 852.

The visitor proceeds down this broad avenue, and a few minutes later finds himself entering the world-famous Piazza. The square is open in front. At the two sides are the curved colonnades of Bernini. The colonnades consist of four rows of columns, 284 columns in all. The spaces between the rows form three covered arcades, the center one of which is large enough to accommodate two automobiles, driving abreast. When the visitor walks under the colonnades he seems to be in a great silent forest of majestic stone columns.

Near the front of the church the colonnades seem to straighten out to form parallel rows of pillars. They were curved before; now they are suddenly straight. There were four rows of pillars on each side; now there are only two. These rows, two on each side of the square, lead to the front of the church.

These avenues of pillars and the colonnades are roofed and are surmounted by 162 colossal statues of saints. The visitor scarcely notices these statues. So vast is the entire square that the statues, big as they are, seem insignificant parts of the magnificent whole.

In the center of the square stands the great obelisk or "needle," which was moved from the site of Nero's circus and erected in its present location in 1586. On top of it is a bronze cross containing a fragment of the true Cross. The monument of the pagans has been "converted" to Christianity and has been given the honor of bearing one of the most precious relics in all the world.

On the ground at each side of the obelisk is a red and white plate. The visitor, standing on one of the plates, sees the four rows of columns in the colonnade as one row, so perfectly have they been placed. Near the plates are the two fountains which the visitor has already observed from a distance. Their water spouts fifteen or twenty feet into the air.

The visitor walks across the great square until he comes to the steps that lead up to the church. On both sides of these steps are the corridors of pillars described above. The area covered by these steps alone is greater than that covered by most churches.

As the visitor climbs the steps he observes the front or façade of the church, the front that was added by Maderna after Michelangelo's death. Students of architecture tell us that the

front is poorly designed and not worthy of such a beautiful
church. The visitor is impressed, however, by the massive columns and by the gigantic statues of Christ, the Blessed Virgin,
and the Apostles that are on the roof. There is a little balcony
over the central entrance upon which the Holy Father appears
on special occasions to give his blessing *Urbi et Orbi* (to the
city and to the world).

The visitor looks up at the balcony and then back over the
square. How many times that square has been packed to its
capacity with people waiting to receive the blessing of the
Holy Father! When the cardinals are gathered in solemn
conclave, thousands of people wait in the square to hear news
of the election of the new Pope. A few minutes after the
name of the new Pontiff has been announced from the balcony,
the Pope himself appears wearing his robes of office for the first
time to give his blessing *Urbi et Orbi.*

It was in this square on that rainy February day in 1929
that the crowds came to cheer Pope Pius XI after the signing
of the Lateran Treaty. Every Easter morning and on many
other occasions the Holy Father appears to give his blessing
and each time the square is packed with eager, cheering people.
The visitor looking back over the vast expanse of pavement
finds it difficult to believe that there could be enough people
in all Rome to fill that space.

For three hundred years, ever since the modern church was
built, the Popes have been appearing on that balcony to give
their blessing. The appearances stopped only during the fifty-
nine years that the Popes were the voluntary prisoners of the
Vatican. Even during that period there was one blessing *Urbi
et Orbi.* Just after Pope Pius XI was elected in 1922 he said,
much to everyone's astonishment, that he wished to appear on
the balcony and give the blessing. This was the first time that
such a thing had happened in half a century. Perhaps it was
a sign of the approaching settlement of the "Roman Question."

So far, the visitor has not been stopped by the Swiss guards or by any other officials of Vatican City. "Why is this?" you may ask. "Are not the Basilica and the Square parts of Vatican City?"

They are parts of Vatican City, but they are parts that are almost always open to the public. Ordinarily the Piazza is under the jurisdiction of the Rome police. It is only on special occasions that the square is closed off and the Vatican police take charge.

Although the church and square are included within the boundaries of the state of Vatican City, they are not considered parts of the Vatican. The latter consists only of the Papal Palace, the Vatican gardens, and the buildings in the gardens. St. Peter's is governed entirely separately. A large number of priests are assigned to St. Peter's and are presided over by a vicar. A corps of architects and a large number of workmen, called the *sanpietrini*, keep the great church and square in constant repair.

The visitor has passed the huge stone statue of St. Peter that stands in front of the church and has reached the porch. Here, it is generally agreed, Maderna created his masterpiece. The porch has a grandeur, a majesty, that is indescribable. The giant columns seem to reach up and up and up, and the visitor feels tiny and insignificant as he stands under them.

Five doors lead into the Basilica. The one on the extreme right is the Holy Door, which is opened only during the Holy Year, proclaimed by the Supreme Pontiff once every twenty-five years. The Holy Door is not really a door at all. It is a slab which fills in the opening. This slab is removed at the beginning of each Holy Year.

The center door is made of bronze and was originally in the old Basilica of St. Peter. It dates from the fifteenth century. On it are depicted scenes in the lives of Christ, the Blessed Virgin, the Apostles, and many of the saints.

Above the door is a gigantic mosaic picture which the Florentine artist Giotto made for the old church in the fifteenth century. In it the Catholic Church is represented as a little ship in which the disciples and our Lord are tossed about upon a wild sea. The winds, represented as human beings, are trying their best to sink the ship but are unsuccessful. The visitor thinks of the words Christ spoke when He founded the Church: "And the gates of hell shall not prevail against it." How true these words have proved! Time and time again the Church has been attacked by powerful enemies and at first these enemies have seemed to meet with great success. In the end, however, each attack has failed and the Church has emerged stronger than it was before.

The great Basilica itself was built on the ruins of the circus where the pagan emperors had put Christian martyrs to death in their determination to stamp out Christianity. How weak the infant Church seemed at that time, how strong the pagan emperors! Today, the only traces of the old empire are those which have been carefully preserved by the Popes.

The Church has its enemies today. It will have more in the future. But these enemies will pass away and be forgotten and the Church will still stand, dripping, perhaps, with the blood of her martyrs, but unbowed. In any struggle between the Church and any other force the result is written in advance.

The visitor, however, has little time to devote to such reflections now. He is eager to see the Basilica. He enters the great central door. The square is an inspiring sight, but it is as nothing compared with what he is about to see.

Chapter XX

ABOVE THE TOMB OF ST. PETER

MERE WORDS cannot do justice to the great Basilica of St. Peter. It must be visited to be appreciated, not once but many times. So vast is it, so rich in treasures of all kinds, that each trip will reveal something that was not seen before.

As the visitor steps through the center door and sees the church for the first time, he knows that it is big; he does not realize how big. Some churches are built in such a way that they look much larger than they are. This is especially true of the Gothic type, because of the sweep of the unbroken lines. In St. Peter's all lines, vertical as well as horizontal, are broken and the effect is just the opposite. It is some time before the visitor realizes the vastness of the edifice.

As he stands near the entrance, he looks across the expanse of pavement toward the main altar which is covered by a great bronze canopy or baldachin as it is called. No pews or chairs obstruct his view. In Italy and in many other countries of Europe, people kneel on the floors of their churches. The nave of the church, which is the part that extends from the entrance to the altar, is supported by five pairs of pillars with four arches between. This also makes the church look smaller. Who could dream that only four arches could span so great a distance! On the other sides of these pillars are side aisles containing chapels, but the visitor scarcely notices them at first. Above the pillars is a cornice which projects from the wall. The cornice does not look at all large, yet it has been said that a man could ride a horse along it with no trouble at all. Above the cornice is the great barrel-vaulted roof of the nave. Everything is richly decorated — the pillars, the walls, the ceiling, even the floor.

The visitor is impressed by the view. Yes, he thinks, St. Peter's is big. Then suddenly he sees something move in front of the main altar. It is a man. But how very, very small he looks! Immediately everything takes on new proportions. If a full-grown man looks so small then the altar behind him must be immense, and how large the central pillars or dome piers must be for they tower over the altar. And the dome of the Basilica rises far, far above the tops of the pillars!

The visitor realizes that his sense of proportion has been all wrong, that everything in this church is much larger than it seems. He takes another look at the "little" cherubs holding the holy water fonts near the entrance and realizes with a start that they are more than six feet in height!

St. Peter's is built in the form of a cross. Because of this, it is impossible to see the entire church at one time. The main altar with its baldachin is at the center of the cross and cuts off the visitor's view no matter in which part of the Basilica he is standing. From the main altar the arms of the cross extend in four different directions.

The longest arm consists of the nave, which extends from the altar to the entrance, and the two aisles which flank it. The word *aisle* used in this sense must not be confused with the passage between rows of pews which we ordinarily call an aisle today. This is a later use of the word. In speaking of St. Peter's we are going back to the original meaning. In St. Peter's, and other old churches of the same type, the nave has two wings running parallel with it, one on each side. They are called aisles. They are separated from the nave by rows of pillars. The roofs over the aisles are much lower than the one over the nave.

The arms of the cross which extend to the right and left of the altar are called transepts. The extension of the nave behind the altar is called the apse. The four arms are connected not only at the center of the church but also by passages around the dome piers. These are pillars that support the dome. They are much larger than the ones that support the roof of the nave. Each of these passages is large enough to accommodate several chapels. Nave, aisle, transept, apse, dome pier — these are all words we must remember as we accompany the visitor on his tour of St. Peter's.

The visitor decides that, first of all, he should like to see the altar and the Confession at the center of the church. From the entrance, therefore, he proceeds down the nave. One of the first sights to greet his eyes is a large disk, or round flat plate, set into the pavement. This formerly stood before the High Altar in the old St. Peter's. The emperors of the Holy Roman Empire knelt upon it when they were crowned.

As the visitor continues forward he sees all about him statues, altars, and tombs of kings, emperors, and Popes. He is now getting a faint idea of the great number of treasures housed in the Basilica.

On the marble pavement of the nave the relative lengths of the principal churches of the world are given. There is a mark on the floor indicating the length of each church as it compares with the length of St. Peter's. St. Paul's in London is about five sixths of the length of St. Peter's. It is 520.3 feet while St. Peter's is 693.8 feet. Other lengths are: the Cathedral of Florence, 492.2; the Cathedral of Milan, 442.2; the Basilica of St. Paul in Rome, 419.2. The world-famous Church of St. Sophia in Constantinople is about half the length of St. Peter's. It is 354 feet long.

The visitor has now reached the main altar over which towers the great baldachin with its twisted bronze columns covered with lavish gold decorations. The baldachin was designed by Bernini, the same architect who designed the colonnades and the statues in front of the church. It was built of bronze. Most of the bronze came from Venice. Some of it came from the Pantheon in Rome. The baldachin is 95 feet high.

To say that the baldachin is 95 feet high may mean very little until you recall that this is the height of the average ten-story building. Picture in your mind a ten-story building that you have seen recently and then imagine an altar with a canopy so high. Then imagine a church so large that this altar and canopy could be placed in the center of it and not seem at all out of proportion.

The altar is reserved for the Mass of the Supreme Pontiff. Light streams in upon it from the great dome of Michelangelo, far, far above. In front of the altar is the Confession of St. Peter, a lowered place in the floor directly over the tomb of the Apostle.

The entire center of the church may be said to form the tomb of St. Peter. The Confession is directly over the tomb of the first Pope, and the main altar is partly over it. The huge dome is over both the Confession and the main altar and forms a roof for the gigantic vault. On each of the four dome piers is a colossal marble statue, and above each statue is a mosaic picture. The statues and the pictures form part of the decorations of the tomb. Above the mosaics and just under the beginning of the dome is a Latin inscription which runs all the way around the center of the church: "Thou art Peter, and upon this rock I will build my church and I will give thee the keys to the kingdom of heaven." The visitor at first judges these letters to be about a foot and a half high. In reality, they are six feet in height.

The statues mentioned above stand in niches in the dome piers. Above each statue is a gallery on which is a repository containing the most precious relics of the saint depicted below. These relics are the handkerchief of Veronica on which our Saviour left an imprint of His face; a fragment of the true Cross found by St. Helena; the spear with which Longinus pierced our Lord's side; and the head of St. Andrew. On special occasions all four of these relics, called the Great Relics, are placed on the gallery of Veronica and displayed to the public.

In the wedge-shaped spaces above the galleries are gigantic mosaic pictures of the evangelists. Some idea of the size of the pictures may be obtained from the fact that the pen in the hand of St. John is five feet long!

The dome rises to a dizzy height above the altar. It is pierced by many windows which focus their light upon the altar and the Confession. The walls of the dome are covered with mosaics and with many other beautiful decorations.

The visitor now goes to the Confession of St. Peter. In front of the altar the floor is lowered in a wide semicircle to a depth of about twelve feet. The space is enclosed by a marble balustrade. A stairway on each side of the semicircle leads down to another altar. This altar is fixed to the wall that supports the main altar above. On the balustrade 89 guilded bronze lamps burn night and day. Relics of St. Peter are kept in niches in the wall under the main altar. They are behind a gilded metal door with twining, pieced leafwork. A white marble statue of Pope Pius VI stands at the foot of the staircases. The Pontiff is represented as kneeling, as he so often prayed before the grave of St. Peter. In a silver vase is kept the white wool from which are made the palliums (bands of white wool marked by four purple crosses) bestowed on Archbishops and Patriarchs. All parts of the Confession, railings, steps, walls, and floors gleam with the most precious stones and metals.

The Confession seems a small, quiet, secluded spot amidst the vastness that surrounds it. Everything inspires devotion: the dim light of the lamps, the knowledge that this spot is directly above the tomb of St. Peter, the statue of the kneeling Pope, and the faithful who are always kneeling on the steps. The visitor drops to his knees and prays fervently. This is the very heart of St. Peter's and the Vatican.

Chapter XXI

EXPLORING THE BASILICA

WHEN THE visitor leaves the Confession of St. Peter to
continue his inspection of the Basilica, he scarcely knows where
to start. He is standing in the center of the church and the four
arms of the cross extend in as many directions. Each section has
its chapels, its tombs, its statues, its pictures. Everywhere there
is something of interest.

The best plan seems to be to start again at the entrance.
Although he has proceeded down the nave on the way to the
altar, he had not inspected the chapels in the aisles. He decides
to explore the right aisle, then proceed around the dome piers,
through the right transept, the apse, the left transept, and then
the left aisle which will bring him back to the entrance
once more.

The right aisle is bordered by four chapels. The first of them
contains Michelangelo's famous statue, the Pietà. The artist
was only twenty-five years old when he chiseled this magnificent
work, and he accomplished it in one year. Mary sits at the foot
of the Cross holding in her lap the body of her Divine Son.
When Michelangelo was older he accomplished larger, more
stupendous works, but nothing that surpassed the Pietà for
its beautiful simplicity, its intense feeling. The dead Saviour's
body, the Mother's face, the surrounding drapes, all are executed
in exquisite detail. The grief and resignation depicted on the
face of the Blessed Virgin are so real that the heart of anyone

who sees this statue goes out to the bereaved Virgin in her anguish.

Only the greatest of sculptors could have put such feeling into cold marble. The visitor stands in front of the statue for some time, and it is with reluctance that he finally leaves to continue his tour.

Next is the chapel of St. Nicholas. Then follows the chapel of St. Sebastian, and, finally, the roomy chapel of the Sacrament. Here is the tomb of Pope Sixtus IV who reigned from 1471 to 1484. This is a bronze monument made by Antonio Pollajoulo in 1493. There is a striking likeness of the Pontiff on the slab, and surrounding it are figures representing theology, philosophy, and the liberal arts. Nothing could be more appropriate, for Pope Sixtus IV was a great patron of learning.

The tomb of Sixtus IV is the oldest in the church proper, although there are older ones in the crypts beneath. The tombs are among the most magnificent works of art in St. Peter's. They are found in all parts of the Basilica. Some rest against the pillars; others are built into large niches in the walls; and others rise like altars from the floor. The tombs are interesting from several standpoints: artistic, religious, historical. Most of them were executed by master architects and represent the best art of the period in which they were erected. It is interesting to note how styles in architecture have changed through the centuries.

Each tomb stirs memories of the Pontiff who is buried there, of his struggles, his defeats, his victories. Each of the Popes has faced great problems, for there has never been a time when the Church has not had formidable enemies. The tomb of Pius VII, for example, recalls that Pontiff's persecution at the hands of Napoleon. Tales of a similar nature could be told of almost all the Popes resting in St. Peter's. Once more the fact is brought home that no purely human institution could have survived the ordeals undergone by the Catholic Church.

In all, 144 Popes are buried in St. Peter's and in the crypts beneath. This is more than half of the 261 Pontiffs who have preceded the present Holy Father on the throne of St. Peter. Many others are buried in other parts of Rome.

In front of the last pillar on the right side of the nave is a bronze statue of St. Peter which is thought to date back to the fourth or fifth century. St. Peter is seated with his hand raised as if in blessing. His right foot projects a little beyond the left, and for centuries it has been the custom of pilgrims to kiss the right foot in veneration. So many times has it been kissed that the toes have been worn away and the bronze foot worn smooth.

Statues of the founders of religious orders stand in niches in the pillars about the church. Marble reliefs of many of the Popes also adorn the pillars.

A passage around the dome piers connects the nave with the right transept. While going through this passage, the visitor sees the Gregorian Chapel named after Pope Gregory XIII who had it decorated according to plans by Michelangelo.

Gregory XIII was the Pope responsible for the reforming of the calendar. The Julian calendar which had been used since the days of Julius Caesar was eleven minutes and twelve seconds too long. By 1578 the calendar year was ten days behind the sun year. In that year most Catholic countries adopted the Gregorian calendar which provided that leap year, instead of occurring every four years, would be omitted in those years divisible by 100 but not in those divisible by 400. In order to make up the ten days which had been lost, the day after October 4, 1578, was called October 15. Millions of persons went to sleep on October 4 and woke up on October 15.

Great Britain, being a Protestant country, refused to follow the lead of the Pope and continued to use the Julian Calendar until 1752. The American colonies, being subject to Great Britain, also used the Julian calendar. When the change was finally made, it was necessary to skip eleven days, for the Julian Calendar had fallen behind another day in the course of two centuries. Although we celebrate Washington's birthday on February 22, he was actually born on February 11 according to the calendar which was used at the time.

In the right transept there are many tombs. Especially noteworthy is that of Countess Matilda of Tuscany, the powerful friend and protector of the Popes, who ruled a large section of central and northern Italy in the eleventh century. There is a statue, carved by Bernini, of the Countess holding the papal tiara and beneath is a carving in relief showing the absolution of Henry IV at Canossa.

This tomb recalls the historic conflict between Pope Gregory VII and Emperor Henry IV of Germany and of the part Countess Matilda played in the struggle. In 1076 Henry had his council declare Gregory was no longer Pope. Gregory retaliated by declaring that no Christian any longer owed allegiance to the emperor. When all his people, including the dukes and lords, deserted him, Henry crossed the Alps in the dead of winter and did public penance at Canossa where the Pope was the guest of Matilda.

Henry's repentance was short-lived. When he renewed the contest, Matilda supported Gregory and his successors, supplying them with men and money. Twice Henry laid waste her lands, but she remained steadfast in her allegiance to the Popes. Finally, Henry was defeated at Canossa, the very place where he had done public penance a few years before. When Matilda died, she left all her lands to the Holy See.

In passing from the right transept to the apse the visitor goes around another dome pier. In the passageway he sees the tomb of Clement XIII which was designed by the great architect Canova and is one of the outstanding tombs of the church.

One of the most massive pieces of work in the Basilica is the repository of the Chair of St. Peter. This monument, designed by Bernini, stands at the rear of the church. The bronze chair in which the original chair is enclosed is upheld by the four great fathers of the church: Saints Ambrose and Augustine in front, Saints Athanasius and Chrysostom in the rear. Above hovers a dove, symbolic of the Holy Ghost. The dove is surrounded by great masses of angels, clouds, and rays of light. The work has been expertly done, although many students of art say that it is much too large.

The chair which St. Peter occupied as head of the Church has been venerated for many centuries as a sacred relic. It is a symbol of the uninterrupted succession of the supreme shepherds. Every January 18 is observed as the Feast of St. Peter's Chair in Rome.

In 1867, the eighteen hundredth anniversary of the death of St. Peter, the chair was moved from its receptacle, and so now it is possible to give a description of it. It is square and very solid-looking. It is made of oak and locust wood, but the parts made of locust wood are thought to date from later times. Four iron rings are fastened to the props, so that by inserting poles the chair could be borne as a sedan chair. Ivory pictures adorn many parts of it, but these, too, are thought to be later additions.

After leaving this impressive monument, the visitor proceeds through the passage around the third dome pier. Here is the monument to Alexander VIII. Here also is the altar of the Madonna della Colonna below which is an early Christian sarcophagus containing the remains of Saints Leo II, Leo III, and Leo IV. A great marble relief of the Retreat of Attilla from Rome is above the altar of Leo I. Farther on is the monument of Alexander VII, opposite which is an oil painting of St. Peter's Basilica by Vareni.

The picture of St. Peter's is unique in that it is the only oil-painted altar piece in the Basilica. All the others are mosaics. The original paintings have been reproduced with infinite patience in tiny bits of colored stones. A mosaic will last thousands of years without losing its color, but the making of one takes so much time, skill, and patience that only the best works of art are reproduced in this way. Of the Vatican mosaic makers we shall learn more in a later chapter.

Many persons go through St. Peter's without realizing that the altar pieces are not oil paintings. It is only under very close inspection and in a certain light that the cracks between the stones can be seen. Some of the original paintings are in the collections of the Vatican and some are in various churches throughout Rome.

In the left transept the visitor finds three altars. The middle one is particularly noteworthy because it marks the spot in the circus of Nero where St. Peter was crucified. The bodies of two Apostles, Simeon and Judas Thaddeus, repose in a stone sarcophagus beneath the altar.

The visitor is particularly impressed by the confessionals in the left transept. Signs inform the faithful that confessions will be heard in eleven different languages. Nothing could better demonstrate the universality of the Catholic Church. Catholics come to Rome from every part of the world. Many of them seem to have nothing in common. Their homelands are entirely dissimilar, as are their customs and their clothes. They cannot talk with one another, for they speak a variety of tongues. Even the color of their skins is different. Yet they are all members of the same great Church, and in St. Peter's all may be absolved from their sins by the Sacrament of Penance.

The visitor's curiosity is aroused by the long rods standing near the confessionals. Upon inquiry he is told that, after giving absolution, the confessor touches the head of the penitent with one of the rods. In ancient Rome a slave, upon receiving his freedom, received also a tap on the head. The tap with the rod signifies freedom from the bondage of sin.

Proceeding on his tour of inspection, the visitor walks through the passage around the fourth dome pier. On the right, under the monument of Pius VII is the entrance to the sacristy.

The visitor now finds himself in the left aisle bordering the nave. Here are three more chapels and the elevator to the roof. The first of the chapels is used for the prayers of the priests who are assigned to St. Peter's. The last is used as a baptistery and the visitor sees a number of babies held in the arms of their godmothers, being baptized at the beautiful font.

This brings the visitor back to the entrance. He has still to visit the crypts beneath the church, the sacristy, and the dome, but he has finished his inspection of the church itself — his first inspection. He knows now that St. Peter's is too vast to be seen in one trip. The first trip has given him only a fleeting over-all glimpse of the great wealth of treasures, spiritual and material, contained in the Basilica. On future visits he will take time to inspect the various parts of the church and will more fully appreciate this great temple of Christianity.

Chapter XXII

ABOVE AND BELOW ST. PETER'S

HAVING COMPLETED his inspection of St. Peter's Basilica
and the Piazza, the visitor has still to see the sacristy of the
famous church, the crypts beneath it, and the dome above it.

The sacristy, or vestry, is a new addition, having been added
to the Basilica in 1775. Anything built as recently as 1775
seems new in the ancient Vatican, yet the entire history of the
United States has taken place since that date — the Declaration
of Independence was not signed until the following year.

The entrance to the sacristy is a long passageway between the
left transept and the left aisle. The sacristy itself contains four
large rooms and many art treasures. The visitor is particularly
interested in the fluted pillars which once adorned the villa
of the pagan emperor Hadrian; the Dalmatic of Charlemagne,
a vestment said to have been worn by Charlemagne when he
was crowned emperor by Pope Leo III; and in the three rows
of candlesticks and candelabra which adorn the Papal altar on
special occasions. There are also valuable chalices, ciboriums,
and a host of other interesting objects.

*   *   *

The entrance to the crypts is near the pier of St. Veronica.
The visitor descends the staircase and finds himself in the horseshoe-shaped passageway of the new crypt. This was built at the
time the new church was erected and is located under the dome.

Proceeding to the left, the visitor finds himself at the chapel of the Tomb of St. Peter. This chapel is under the main altar and the Confession and occupies the spot where once stood the oratory, the little church that was built over the tomb of St. Peter by Anacletus, the third Pope. The chapel was built at the order of Pope Clement VIII, one of the last persons to see the tomb of St. Peter. It is very small and is built in the form of an inverted cross to commemorate the tradition that St. Peter was crucified head downward because he declared he was not worthy to be crucified as his Saviour had been. The chapel has an arched studio roof with panels portraying various miracles. The altar is almost directly over the tomb and is approached by three steps. The carpet in front of the altar has woven upon it the words *Principi Apost* (To the Prince of the Apostles). Above the altar is a mosaic of Saints Peter and Paul. The decorations are anything but lavish and not to be compared with those in the Basilica above. Everything in the church itself is built around the tomb of St. Peter. The altar and the Confession are directly over it. The great baldachin which is above it is the most prominent thing in the church. The lights from the dome shine down upon it. The decorations of the piers face the tomb, and the four arms of the cross lead into it.

In contrast, the visitor comes upon the chapel which is over the tomb of St. Peter almost before he knows it. The chapel is so small, so secluded, so simple that it inspires a feeling of awe and reverence in the visitor. He falls to his knees and prays to St. Peter, just as he did in the Confession. Now he is even closer to the tomb, as close as it is possible for anyone to get. The chapel reminds him of St. Peter himself, the humble, unpretentious fisherman.

When, at length, the visitor takes his leave of this sacred shrine, he finds himself at the sarcophagus of Junius Bassus, which is opposite the entrance to the chapel. This is the most magnificent of the early Christian tombs. Junius Bassus was

Prefect of Rome in A.D. 359. He became a convert while Prefect and died the same year.

Adjoining the horseshoe-shaped passageway are a number of chapels containing remarkable works of art from the old Basilica. The visitor inspects many of them and then proceeds to the old crypt. This is the remains of old St. Peter's and is located under the nave. The floor of the new church is about seven feet higher than that of the old one, and the space between forms the old crypt.

Eighty-six Popes were buried in the old Basilica, but many of the tombs were damaged or destroyed when the church was torn down. Many emperors, cardinals, and other important persons are also buried there.

The visitor finds the tomb of Nicholas V particularly interesting. About the time that Christopher Columbus was born, Nicholas V was making his plans for transforming the Vatican into a Papal city. It was he who started the work of building the new Basilica. It was he who founded the Vatican library. Few men have left so pronounced a mark upon the Vatican.

Adrian IV, the only Englishman who ever sat upon the throne of St. Peter, rests in a gigantic sarcophagus of red Egyptian granite. The only inscription is *Hadriano Papa IV*.

New excavations are being made under the Basilica at the present time. When a place was prepared for the tomb of Pope Pius XI, a hidden chapel was revealed by the removal of a wall. It was immediately decided that further excavations should be made. Two underground passages have thus far been found. They are believed to be part of the old pagan tombs which were once located on Vatican Hill and among which St. Peter was buried. Many ruins of Nero's circus have been found. Both the old and the new Basilicas have been erected on the remains of this circus. It is hoped that in the future even more interesting discoveries will be made, but excavation is proceeding slowly because of the limited funds available for the work.

Galloway

The
Laocoon
Group.

A mural by Raphael in the Vatican.

St. Peter's
Dome from the
Ethiopian
College.

Press Assn.

Clerical students leaving the Ethiopian College.

The Vatican Power House is modern in every respect.

Vatican Railroad Station. (below) Vatican Radio Station.

Clerical students from the Augustinian house of studies (Irish branch) broadcasting over the Vatican Radio.

Control room of the Vatican Radio.

St. Peter's lighted up at night.

The wall surrounding the Vatican City is as impressive as its buildings.

Fountains
play in the
Piazza of
St. Peter's.

Press Assn.

Lt. Gen. Mark W. Clark, Fifth Army Commander, rides through
Rome June 5, 1944, day after its liberation.

Pope Pius XII blesses American war correspondents in the Vatican, June 7,

Press Assn.

The visitor proceeds on his way examining tomb after tomb. At length he re-enters the new crypt where he sees more chapels and more works of art and eventually finds himself back at the steps which lead to the Basilica. He realizes that a student could spend weeks in the crypts studying the remains of the Basilica of Constantine.

*   *   *

Having spent some time under the Basilica, the visitor decides to go to the dome which towers over it. Near the entrance he steps into a spacious elevator which takes him to the roof of the nave. The roof is a large flat expanse with many cupolas and a few houses in which guards live. The visitor looks with great interest at the Piazza below, the superb colonnades, the broad avenue leading to the Tiber, the Castel Sant'Angelo, the city of Rome, and the blue mountains behind.

When he is on the roof, however, the visitor has scarcely begun his climb. The dome rises three hundred and eight feet above the roof. The dome has an outer and an inner shell and the staircase is between the two shells. The climb is a great one. The visitor stops now and then to get his breath.

A gallery runs around the dome near the top. Peering over the railing at the abyss below makes the visitor dizzy. The great ten-story-high baldachin looks the size of a living-room clock.

The gallery looks down into the Vatican gardens, and the people walking about in them seem like dwarfs. From here can be seen the majestic size of the Papal Palace with its huge courts. The entire city of Rome can be seen and also many suburban towns. The sea looks like a silver streak in the distance.

A ladderlike staircase leads to the inside of the ball that is between the cupola and the cross. This is a sort of hollow copper globe. Only about twenty persons at a time are admitted to it. It sways about very uncomfortably, and the visitor is only too glad to go back to the gallery.

*   *   *

There is one sight which the visitor will not see no matter how long he remains in Rome: the lighting of the façade and the dome by the *sanpietrini*, or workmen of St. Peter's. This colorful custom was discontinued in 1939 when a new system of reflected lighting was introduced.

Before this, however, in June, 1935, when Saints John Fisher and Thomas More were canonized, George Barnard, staff correspondent of the N.C.W.C. News Service, gave the following vivid description of the lighting:

"St. Peter's was ablaze last night with myriads of flickering lights, and two saints have been added to the calendar. This is the first time St. Peter's, in all its long history, has been afire to signal the glory of men of our tongue. The Basilica was being built when John Fisher was Bishop of Rochester, and Thomas More, afterward England's Lord Chancellor, was a member of England's Parliament. It is 400 years since they died, and during those 400 years their luster has remained undimmed.

"The sight of St. Peter's outlined by dancing fire is one of the sights of the world. There is nothing quite like it. The lights of New York's Broadway are dead compared with it. . . .

"I had never before seen this sight. No photograph can convey the slightest impression of its beauty, as no photograph can show the beauty of the sea. Breezes sweep across the lights like the wind making waves on a cornfield. And, when the breeze rests, the lights, seen from a distance and an eminence, scintillate like the facets of a great diamond.

"The actual lighting of the dome is the greatest marvel. Tallow candles in vellum lamps were lighted on the façade before dark. When dusk fell, the Roman sky was turned to blue velvet, the lights burned clear, and Rome awaited the lighting of the dome.

"Men and women crowded the Tiber bridges. Crowds were on the Pincio Terrace. People from the villages stood waiting on the hills.

"The first stroke of nine boomed out on the clock of St. Peter's. At once swarms of little black figures crowded out on the top of the dome and clambered down like spiders. As they went torch in hand, they swung to right and left touching the wicks of the waiting tallow candles, weaving a web of light.

"And before the final stroke of nine rang out over the Piazza the job was done. The people cheered."

The "little black figures" were the *sanpietrini*, the workmen of St. Peter's. Most of their fathers were Vatican workers before them, and their grandfathers, and their great grandfathers, back into the centuries. So skilled are they that it is rarely necessary to call in outside workmen for even the most difficult and unusual tasks.

Many persons who had watched the picturesque ceremony of the lighting of the dome felt a pang of regret when it was announced that in the future the lighting would be done by means of reflectors. The reflected lighting is very beautiful, however. The dome sends forth flashes of brilliance which give an effect very similar to the dancing lights of the candles. Moreover, the church can now be lighted in any kind of weather. In the old days, the Holy Father would not permit the lighting to take place if any rain had fallen a short time previously. So great was his concern for the workmen that he would not permit them to climb about on the wet dome.

PART VII
The Papal Palace

Chapter XXIII

THE HOME OF THE POPE

THE PAPAL Palace, which has been the official residence of the Popes since the fourteenth century, is so vast that no one knows all its corners. No one even knows exactly how many rooms there are in the Palace, although the number is approximately one thousand.

Every Pope has left his imprint on the Palace. As the need arose additions were made and the old parts were altered. Roofs were raised; halls were divided; new doorways were cut; old doors were closed. Today, there are halls that lead into blank walls. There are three or four levels on one floor.

Despite the lack of uniformity the general effect is far from displeasing. The various rooms, the chapels, the courtyards, the staircase, almost everything in the Palace, is beautiful. Under the direction of the Popes scores of the world's best architects and artists have had a hand in its decorating.

A section of the Palace can be seen from St. Peter's Square, rising behind the colonnade of Bernini. The part that contains the Pope's apartments can be seen from there as can the Sistine Chapel and the Galleries of Raphael. The best view of the exterior, however, can be obtained from the cupola of St. Peter's.

From there the Palace is seen not as one building but as a collection of connected buildings interspersed by many courtyards.

Near St. Peter's are a large number of courts surrounded in irregular fashion by a group of buildings. These buildings are all part of the Palace and contain the Pope's apartments, the apartments of the Secretary of State, the Sistine Chapel, the Pauline Chapel, the Royal Hall, the Royal Staircase, the chapel of Nicholas V, the chapel of Matilda, the Galleries of Raphael, the Chambers of Raphael, the Borgia Apartments, and many other places of great interest. It is with this section of the Palace chiefly that this chapter will deal.

Behind this group of buildings a person standing on the cupola of the Basilica sees two long narrow parallel wings. These wings were originally connected only at the two ends and enclosed a giant courtyard. Within recent centuries they have been connected by two lateral wings which have divided the original court into three parts. The first of these lateral wings contains the greatest part of the Vatican library. The other is the Braccio Nuovo, or New Wing, and contains part of one of the Vatican museums.

Of the three courts enclosed by these wings, the one closest to St. Peter's is the beautiful Belvedere Court. The farthest from St. Peter's is the Court of the Pine, so called because it contains a huge sculptured pine cone from old St. Peter's. The small center one is called the Court of the Printing House because until 1909 it served as the home of the Vatican printing presses.

These wings and the small group of buildings behind them are devoted almost entirely to the library and the museums. They will be dealt with in succeeding chapters.

The visitor seeking an audience with the Holy Father enters the Palace by means of the bronze gate near the Basilica. He presents his audience card to the Swiss guards stationed there.

This card can be obtained from the Papal Chamberlain, at present Monsignor Arborio-Mella di Sant' Elia Alberto.

Opposite the bronze gate is the beginning of the vast stone stairway designed by Bernini, the Scala Regia, or Royal Stairs. This staircase is reserved for princes and sovereigns who are on their way to assist at the Pope's Mass in the Sistine Chapel. On the first landing is a large statue of Constantine mounted on a horse. Opposite the statue is a door which opens to the porch of St. Peter's. Every twenty-five years, the Pope passes through this door to open the Holy Door which leads into the Basilica. This marks the beginning of another Holy Year.

The great majority of visitors climb the Scala Pia, named after Pope Pius IX who enclosed the stairs. Halfway up is the office of the Papal Chamberlain, and at the top are the apartments of the Maggiordomo. The steps lead to the Court of St. Damasus. This is one of twenty courts in the Palace grounds, but it is a very important one. It is faced by the apartments of the Pope, the Papal Secretary of State, and many other Vatican officials. Of the 1000 rooms in the Palace only about 200 are used as residences, and most of these center about the Court of St. Damasus.

The side of the court which faces St. Peter's is open. The Palace encloses the other three sides and on each of these sides three tiers of galleries look down upon the court. These galleries, or loggias, as they are called, were designed by Bramante and completed by Raphael after the former's death. They are sometimes called the Loggias of Bramante but more often they are referred to as the Loggias of Raphael.

The galleries are supported by pillars on the sides facing the court. Originally these sides were open, but in 1813 Pope Pius VII enclosed them in glass. This detracted from their appearance somewhat, but it was necessary; for the loggias contain many paintings by Raphael and his pupils and their colors were being faded by the weather.

The official entrance of the Palace opens upon the Court of
St. Damasus and is guarded by a Papal gendarme. The visitor
passes through this entrance and climbs more stairs to the Hall
of Pope Clement VIII. In this hall, richly decorated with murals
depicting the life of St. Clement, the visitors await their
audience. At length the *sediari*, men dressed in red damask
velvet, usher the visitors into the Throne Room or into the
Pope's study.

The large audiences are held in the Throne Room which
contains the Papal throne, a gift from the city of Venice. The
Holy Father often receives several hundred persons at a time,
and has received as many as fifteen thousand persons in one day.
The people stand, waiting expectantly, until the Holy Father
enters the room. When he walks in they applaud and shout
"Viva il Papa!" ("Long live the Pope!"). This is astonishing to
an American Catholic who would expect a hushed silence to
fall over the crowd. In Italy, however, customs are different
from those in the United States. This certainly does not mean
that the Italians are any less religious than Americans. This is
their way of showing their affection for the Holy Father.

The Pontiff mounts the steps in front of his throne and the
people fall to their knees while he gives them his blessing. Next
prayer books and rosaries are held out for the Papal blessing.
The blessings having been bestowed, the Holy Father walks
through the crowd allowing everyone to kiss his ring. Often
he stops to talk with some of the people.

It is easier to see the Pope than it is to see almost any president or monarch. Anyone visiting Rome can secure an audience
card with very little difficulty.

Private audiences are held in the Pope's study. Here the Holy
Father discusses affairs of Church and State with his visitors.
It is at his desk in this room that the Pope does most of his work.

The Pope's study is one of 18 rooms in his apartment. This
apartment was completely renovated in 1939 shortly after the

election of Pope Pius XII. The floors of the principal rooms are in polychrome marble which is not an uncommon flooring in Rome. The floor of the drawing room has in its center the coat of arms of the present Pontiff. The inner rooms have floors of wood. The walls are of oiled tinted stucco, and in the frieze that runs around the ceiling the papal coat of arms, a dove and an olive branch frequently appear.

The chapel which was formerly near the Pope's bedroom overlooking the piazza of St. Peter has been moved to another side of the apartment and now looks down upon one of the smaller courts. The walls of the chapel are hung with red damask.

At the time of the renovation the great attics of the Pope's apartments were divided into eleven small compartments. They will be used by some of the cardinals during the next conclave. Even since the recent remodeling the Pope's rooms are among the simplest in the Vatican. The Popes have taken great pride in decorating the other parts of the Vatican for the glory of the Church. For themselves they have done very little.

Directly under the Pope's apartment are the rooms of the Secretary of State. Here the man who is sometimes called the Pope's assistant lives and works and here he receives twice weekly the diplomats accredited to the Vatican.

The few other persons who live in the Palace all have their rooms in this same section at the right of the Court of St. Damasus.

Across the court are many rooms, apartments, and chapels which are world famous. Here are the Borgian Apartments and the Chambers of Raphael, both of which will be described in a later chapter. Here, at the top of the royal stairs is the Sala Regia, or Royal Room, which is also called the Hall of Seven Doors. It is famous for its murals by Vasari. At one time ambassadors and kings were received in this room. It is one hundred feet long, fifty feet wide, and seventy feet high.

One of the seven doors leads into the beautiful and famous Sistine Chapel. It is here that all Papal ceremonies and functions are held, and it is here that the cardinals gather to elect a new Pope. A beautiful marble balustrade separates the part in front reserved for the Pope and the cardinals from that reserved for the laity. Michelangelo's famous painting of the Last Judgment covers the rear wall, and the ceiling was also painted by this great artist. Works by many other outstanding artists adorn the side walls. On the right wall is the box occupied by the choir. A staircase at the rear of the chapel leads down to St. Peter's.

A door in the wall that contains the Last Judgment opens into the Treasury of the Sistine Chapel. This is a part of the Vatican that is little known and is rarely seen by visitors. It contains vestments for the Pope and the cardinals, the Pope's tiaras, decorations for the altar, and countless other objects of great interest.

Another of the seven doors of the Royal Hall opens into the Sala Ducale, a narrow, long, low room constructed by Bernini. The Pope and Cardinals pass through this room on their way to St. Peter's after vesting in the Sala del Pappagallo and Sala dei Paramenti, two rooms that are near by.

Still another of the seven doors leads to a passageway over the porch of St. Peter's. The Holy Father passes through it when he goes to the balcony of St. Peter's to give his blessing *Urbi et Orbi*.

The Pauline Chapel is also reached by means of one of the seven doors. This Chapel is named after Pope Paul III who had it built in 1540. It contains two large paintings by Michelangelo — the Conversion of Paul and the Crucifixion of Peter. Before the opening of the conclave at which a Pope is to be elected, the cardinals assemble in the Sistine Chapel. They hear a sermon in which they are reminded of their sacred obligation to choose an able leader as quickly as possible.

In all, there are seven chapels in the Palace. Besides the Pauline and Sistine Chapels, already named, there are the chapels of Countess Matilda, Nicholas V, Innocent III, Julius III, and Urban VIII. In the other parts of the Vatican there are six churches. St. Ann's, the parish church, is at the right of the Piazza near the barracks of the Swiss guards. There are also the churches of St. Giles, St. Martha, St. Stephen, St. Martin (which is the chapel of the Swiss guards), and St. Peregrine. This brings the total number of churches and chapels within the Vatican to thirteen, and if St. Peter's is added with its great number of chapels, the number is increased greatly. There are more churches and chapels within the confines of Vatican City than in any similar area in the entire world.

The visit to the Pauline Chapel concludes our tour of the parts of the Vatican which border the Court of St. Damasus. They comprise the section which is commonly associated with the Holy Father, the Secretary of State, and the College of Cardinals. They are the parts which are reached by means of the bronze door.

In order to visit the library and the museums it is necessary to go back through the bronze door, across St. Peter's Square, and around to the new gate on the west side of the Vatican.

Chapter XXIV

THE VATICAN LIBRARY

VISITORS FROM the United States should feel perfectly at home in the Vatican Library, for it is the most American of all the great libraries of Europe. When Pope Pius XI decided to modernize it, he sent Monsignor Eugene Tisserant to the United States to visit the leading libraries and to study their methods. After making his report to the Holy Father he was given a free hand to reorganize the library along American lines. Four of the leading library authorities of the United States spent several months at the Vatican aiding in the work, and the Carnegie Foundation also cooperated. At the same time four members of the Vatican library staff went to the United States and worked in the Library of Congress and in the libraries of Columbia University and the University of Michigan.

Seven miles of steel shelving, made in America, were installed to accommodate the great number of books. The most modern lighting system was introduced. A catalog system formed from cards of the Library of Congress was worked out almost entirely according to the American library code. The cards have been placed in row after row of steel index files also made in America. A new ventilating system preserves the books by keeping the air from becoming too moist. Thus the Vatican library, which contains the oldest manuscripts in the world, has been made completely modern.

In the early Christian centuries the Popes saw the necessity of preserving documents and other important papers and set aside a room for this collection. Unfortunately, most of these papers were lost during the numerous invasions of the Eternal City. The present library dates back to 1450 when Pope Nicholas V gathered together 9000 manuscripts which had been scattered about his palace and set aside several rooms for them.

During the years the library continued to grow. Pope Sixtus IV added a great number of manuscripts to the collection. By 1587 the library had grown so much that Pope Sixtus V had to build a new home for it. This was a new wing which joined the two long wings of the Palace and cut the Belvedere Court in two. This wing was beautifully decorated and still bears the name Sistine library although the library has overflowed into many other parts of the Palace.

The most precious manuscripts are still kept in the large hall that was the original library of Sixtus V. Today, however, it looks more like a museum, for it contains many precious gifts which have been given to the Popes.

On December 22, 1931, the roof of this room crashed, destroying the beautiful vaulted ceiling. Pope Pius XI had a narrow escape from death, for he had visited the Sistine library only ten minutes before. One man was killed. The roof crashed through the floor into the reference room below and on down to the basement. Very few books or manuscripts were damaged, but some other valuable treasures were destroyed.

Under Pope Pius XI the Vatican library reached its golden age. During his reign, as we have seen, the library was completely reorganized and modernized. Under him a library school was opened for the training of girls for the task of cataloging the treasures of the library. This set aside an old Vatican tradition. Women had never before been employed in the Vatican.

Pope Pius XI had been a librarian before he became Pope. He was Prefect of the Ambrosian Library in Milan and was later Prefect of the Vatican library. He continued to take a great interest in the latter after his election as Pope.

The Vatican library is primarily a manuscript library and in this respect is the finest in the world. It contains more than 50,000 manuscripts mostly in Latin, but many in Greek, Syriac, and other languages. Among the priceless manuscripts is the *De Republica* of Cicero, probably the oldest Latin manuscript known. It was lost to the world for many years until an official of the library found it in 1822. It was written on parchment and so faded that it was barely legible. By means of a gallnut preparation the manuscript was revived.

There is a pamphlet in the library entitled "In Defense of the Seven Sacraments" which was written by King Henry VIII before he broke away from the Church. The pamphlet was presented to the Pope by the king. It was written in answer to the attacks of Martin Luther. For the writing of it the Pope named Henry "Defender of the Faith." Although Henry left the Church soon after that and took most of England with him, he still chose to retain that title. The kings of England bear it to this day although the king must swear that he is a Protestant on the day of his coronation.

The most valuable manuscript in the library is the *Codex Vaticanus,* a Septuagint Bible of the early fourth century. The Septuagint is the translation of the Old Testament into popular Greek spoken in Egypt. The original Septuagint was completed in 130 B.C. At that time two fifths of the population of Egypt were Jews who had forgotten their Hebrew, and for them the Greek version was made.

In the Vatican library are manuscripts by Virgil, Dante, Martin Luther, Terrence, Tacitus, and many others. There are autographs of Tasso, Michelangelo, Raphael, Luther, Henry VIII, Petrarch, and Thomas Aquinas. There are many items that are valuable only as curiosities. A letter from the Emperor of Burma to Pope Pius IX has been kept because it is enclosed in an elephant's tooth.

The archives formed the beginning of the Vatican library.

For a long time they were not open to the public, and many persons hostile to the Church maintained that the Church was afraid to allow them to be seen. Pope Leo XIII, however, declared, "The Church needs nothing but the truth" and threw the archives open to scholars. Today they are still called the Secret Archives, although there is nothing secret about them. These documents are rich with history and contain much information that could be found nowhere else in the world. Scholars spend many hours a day poring over these ancient records.

One of the most interesting parts of the library is the laboratory where ancient manuscripts ravaged by time are restored. This "manuscript hospital" was started at the end of the nineteenth century and is the most advanced in the world. The late John Pierpont Morgan, the American millionaire, sent to it fifty-six Coptic manuscripts which had been found buried in the sands of upper Egypt. For ten years the Vatican "hospital" worked on them. Now the manuscripts are as good as when they were written, many centuries ago. With Mr. Morgan's permission the Vatican made perfect photographic reproductions for the use of its own scholars.

The library contains a museum of Christian antiquities, a pagan museum, a museum of coins, a collection of gems, a hall of Latin papyrus documents, and two rooms where messages sent by the Popes are kept. There are 350,000 prints and engravings.

In this discussion of the Vatican library there has been no mention of books, usually the most important part of any library. The Vatican library has books — 350,000 of them — but most of them are used in the study of manuscripts. Readers who wish to refer only to books are not encouraged to use the library, for there are many other collections of books in Rome. It is the great number and the quality of its manuscripts that make the Vatican library unique among the libraries of the world.

Chapter XXV

THE ART TREASURES OF THE VATICAN

NO TRIP to the Vatican is complete without a visit to the museums. The collection of art treasures gathered within these museums is one of the most valuable in the world. Such a variety is included that there is something to interest everyone, even those not ordinarily interested in art.

The origin of the Vatican museums can be traced back to the year 1506. In that year a large statue was discovered near the baths of Titus in Rome. This statue, which was carved in the second or third century B.C., is the now famous Laocoon group. Laocoon, according to Greek mythology, was a priest of the god Apollo. He lived in Troy while that city was being besieged by the Greeks. He had committed a crime which had angered some of the gods. One day while he and his two sons were standing in front of the sacrificial altar, two huge serpents came up and wrapped their coils about the three. Escape was impossible. All three died a horrible death because of the crime of the father.

The statue depicts the group just as the father has received the fatal bite in his left side. His entire body is convulsed with pain as he falls back upon the altar, and one can almost hear his deep, agonized groan. The younger son has also just received the death bite, and is in the act of expiring. The older son tries to hold off the serpent, and looks imploringly at his father for the help that will never come. The terrible torture being endured by the three is reflected by every muscle in their bodies.

What the proper pair of hands can do with a piece of stone! No more dissimilar works could be found than the Laocoon group and Michelangelo's Pietà, which the visitor saw in St. Peter's. Yet each is a masterpiece in its own way. One depicts the terrible vengeance of the pagan gods; the other the compassion of the Christian God who died that we might be saved. One is all movement; the other is quiet as death itself. One vividly portrays terrible physical torture; the other portrays something even more difficult to put into stone, the unutterable grief of a mother holding in her arms the body of her crucified Son.

At one time each of these statues was a large unshapen mass of stone awaiting the hands of the master sculptor to transform it into something which would be the marvel of future generations. But how seldom, in the course of centuries, do we find such a master sculptor!

Julius II, who was Pope when the Laocoon group was found, bought the statue from its finder for six hundred pieces of gold. He arranged a special room for it in the Belvedere Palace.

This was the beginning of the Vatican museums. Other celebrated art works were brought to the Vatican and placed in the halls and gardens and in Raphael's loggias. Soon there was not sufficient room for them in these places, so Pope Clement XIV started special museum rooms in the Palace. This work was continued by his successor Pius IV. Today the largest collection of antiquities in the Vatican, the Pio-Clementino Museum, bears the names of both these Popes.

Even though it is pagan art, the Laocoon group occupies a place of honor in the Vatican, the heart of Christianity. The Popes have collected art of all kinds, pagan as well as Christian. So complete is the collection that the *Catholic Encyclopedia* says: "The Papal palaces possess so great an abundance of masterpieces of all ages for the instruction and enjoyment of both the friends and enemies of the Papacy that, were all the other collections of the world destroyed by some catastrophe, the Vatican collection would suffice for the perpetuation of all aesthetic culture, both pagan and Christian."

The six principal museums of the Vatican, not including those which are part of the library, are (1) the Pio-Clementino Museum; (2) the Chiaramonti Museum; (3) the Egyptian Museum; (4) the Etruscan Museum; (5) the Pinacotheca; and (6) the Gallery of Modern Paintings.

The Pio-Clementino Museum is a collection of antique art. It occupies eleven rooms and the Belvedere Court. The Laocoon group is in one of the halls facing the court. The famous Torso of Hercules is also in this collection. The arms, head, and legs of this statue have long been lost, but even so it is rated one of the best bits of ancient sculpture ever discovered. It dates from the first century before Christ. The statue of Apollo, the Greek god, is also world-famous. It would be impossible, however, to go on and name all the well-known pieces of art in this collection.

One of the most interesting rooms to the ordinary visitor is the Hall of Animals. It is quite a surprise to come upon this collection after looking at hundreds of statues of orators, emperors, and gods standing majestically upon their pedestals. Here, suddenly, all is life and movement. An eagle is devouring its prey. A hound is leaping upon a deer. Watchdogs are standing guard. An elephant is having a bell hung around its neck. There is also more color in this room than in most of the others. A lion is carved in brown stone, a lobster in greenish marble, and many of the other animals are portrayed in very realistic colors.

The Chiaramonti Museum was founded by Pope Pius VII and is named after him. Chiaramonti was his family name. Like the Pio-Clementino Museum, it is a collection of antiquities. Ancient objects of all kinds are found here. No fragment has been too small to keep. Many pieces have no artistic value but are of great help to historians trying to reconstruct the lives and habits of people who lived in bygone ages.

On the tombstone of an oil dealer is depicted a press which was used in extracting oil from olives. The press is pictured in such detail that it is possible to tell exactly how it was constructed. On other gravestones are pictured ancient mills, workshops, homes, and many other details of ancient life which would have been lost to us if it were not for collections such as this one. From the tombstones it is even possible to determine what games were played by the boys and girls of ancient Rome.

The *Braccio Nuovo*, or New Wing, is an important part of the Chiaramonti collection. This is one of the two wings which cross the huge court in the center of the Vatican Palace. The other is the Sistine library. The *Braccio Nuovo* is a beautiful building with a vaulted ceiling supported by costly columns of marble, granite, and alabaster. The floor is composed of ancient Roman mosaics. While other parts of the Chiaramonti Museum contain much that is of little artistic value, only the very best works of art have been placed in the *Braccio Nuovo*. Many of the ancient statues and busts found here are world-famous.

The Egyptian Museum was also founded by Pope Pius VII, although it was not opened until 1838 in the pontificate of Gregory XVI. The museum has ten halls full of statues, sarcophagi, mummies, sacred animals, papyrus manuscripts, and numerous other objects from ancient Egypt.

The Etruscan Museum is directly above the Egyptian Museum. The Etruscans lived in central Italy before the coming of the Romans, so it is very appropriate that in Rome there should be an Etruscan Museum. These ancient people had a custom of burying all of a man's possessions with him when he died, and so the Etruscan graves have yielded an invaluable collection of objects of every description. From them it is possible to form a fairly complete picture of the lives and customs of the Etruscans.

The armies of Napoleon confiscated many paintings from the Vatican and from the churches of the Papal States. After the defeat of Napoleon these paintings were returned to the Vatican and Pius VII formed them into the nucleus of a special collection. This is the Pinacotheca or Picture Gallery. At first it was lodged in the Borgia Apartments but it has been moved several times. Each succeeding Pope has added many paintings to this gallery. Pope Pius XI housed it in a new building specially erected for the purpose. It is the only museum not contained in the Papal Palace. The building has been called "the greatest blind building of the twentieth century" — blind because it contains no windows. By using only artificial lighting the paintings are shown to their best advantage and protected from the ravages of the sunlight. Only paintings of outstanding value are contained in the Pinacotheca. Raphael, Leonardo da Vinci, Fra Angelico, Murillo, Titian, Paulo Veronese — these are but a few of the famous artists who are represented there.

The glory of the Church is pictured in the Gallery of Modern Paintings. Most of the pictures here depict saints who have been canonized within the past century. One huge picture portrays Pius IX in the act of promulgating the doctrine of the Immaculate Conception.

*   *   *

Not all the art treasures of the Vatican are contained in the museums or in the library. The Sistine Chapel, as we have seen, contains great paintings by Michelangelo and other masters. The chapel of Nicholas V and the chapel of Pius V contain rare masterpieces. The Galleries or Loggias of Raphael are world-famous for their decorations, among which are many scenes from the Bible painted by the master himself and called "Raphael's Bible."

In the same year that Columbus discovered America, Alexander VI of the Spanish family of Borgia became Pope. He took six rooms on the first floor of the Palace for his residence and had them decorated by the best artists of the time. Ever since, they have been known as the Borgia Apartments.

The rooms were not used by the Popes for a very long time. Later, they were occupied for a time by the cardinal nephews, or secretaries of state as they came to be called. After that they were largely neglected for many years, being used only as a conclave when the cardinals were meeting to elect a Pope. The rooms suffered greatly at the hands of French soldiers when Napoleon's armies occupied Rome. For a while they served as the Pinacotheca and for a while they housed the library.

Pope Leo XIII decided to restore these rooms to their original beauty. This was a formidable undertaking. It meant closing doors which had been cut through the walls, reopening old doors, repairing the plaster, restoring the old paintings, and a number of other tasks requiring almost infinite patience. In 1897 the rooms were opened to visitors and are now used for no other purpose than to display their beauty. The decorations include paintings by Giovanni da Udine, Pinturicchio, and other famous artists of the time. There are scenes in the life of Christ, a life-like figure of Alexander VI, and scenes from the lives of many saints. One entire room is devoted to figures representing the liberal arts.

The Chambers of Raphael or the Stanze di Raffaello are directly above the Borgia Apartments. When the Popes left the Borgia Apartments, they moved to the rooms above them. Several artists were given the task of decorating the rooms, among whom was the young Raphael Sanzio. Pope Julius II was so impressed by Raphael's work that he soon put him in complete charge of the decorating. The task was too much for one man to do by himself, so Raphael did all the sketches, and many of the paintings were completed by his assistants and pupils. All these paintings have been given good care and are in an excellent state of preservation.

How often the name of Raphael comes up when one is speaking of the Vatican! There is one room devoted to tapestries designed by Raphael and his pupils. This room is called the Galleria degli Arazzi. The tapestries are called the Arazzi because they were made at the little town of Arras in Belgium.

Raphael made the sketches, or cartoons, for ten of these tapestries in 1515 and 1516. They were sent to Belgium to the professional tapestry makers of Arras where they were beautifully executed. At first they were hung in the lower part of the Sistine Chapel. When they were beheld for the first time, people gasped over their beauty. No expense had been spared in their making. Gold was used in all of them. The tapestries are considered by many to be Raphael's masterpieces. They represent scenes from the life of Christ and from the history of the early Church. For some reason no one requested the return of the original sketches by Raphael. Seven of them were purchased by King Charles I of England and are now in the South Kensington Museum.

Twelve of the tapestries were sketched by Raphael's pupils and five were done later. Altogether there are twenty-seven tapestries in the Galleria degli Arazzi. The best, by far, are those designed by the master himself.

The tapestries did not adorn the Sistine Chapel for long. During the Sack of Rome — how often that infamous event enters into any story of the Vatican — they were carried away. A French nobleman obtained them and returned them to the Pope in 1553. In 1798 the French soldiers of Napoleon seized and sold them. The purchaser burned parts of them in a vain effort to extract the gold. Ten years later they were repurchased and returned to Pope Pius VII. At that time they were placed in the long hall which they still adorn.

In the course of their travels much of the original beauty of the tapestries has been lost. The brilliant colors have faded, and the gold is tarnished. One has to imagine how they must have gleamed and sparkled in bygone days. Even in their present condition, they rank among the best art works of the Vatican.

No discussion of the art of the Vatican would be complete without a mention of the Studio of Mosaics, one of the few industries of Vatican City. The studio was started in the sixteenth century and was given a new home near the railway station by Pope Pius XI.

It is intensely interesting to watch a mosaic maker at work. He stands in front of a frame or an easel and fits each tiny piece of stone or glass into a bed of cement. Each piece must join the edges of the pieces next to it with delicate exactness. By the worker's side is the picture he is copying. He consults it constantly. It takes several years to make even a small mosaic, and some of those above the altars of St. Peter's took as long as twenty years. When all the pieces have been placed, the mosaic is put into a kiln and baked. After that the work of polishing takes place.

There is a carefully catalogued set of colored stone pieces in the Studio. More than 11,000 shades are represented. Even so, it is sometimes necessary to find new shades for certain pictures.

There would not be enough great pictures in Rome to decorate all the altars of St. Peter's, so mosaics have been made of paintings which hang in churches throughout Italy. These mosaics can be exposed to light indefinitely without being harmed. In fact, they will actually be improved over a period of centuries. Oil paintings, on the other hand, have to be constantly protected from the sunlight.

The Holy Father often presents mosaics as gifts to royalty or to churches. In 1929 Pope Pius XI presented a mosaic reproduction of Murillo's Immaculate Conception to the National Shrine of the Immaculate Conception in Washington, D. C. The figures in this work are larger than life size.

Tapestries represent almost as much work as mosaics. There is a group of nuns in the Vatican who have devoted their lives to the repairing and making of tapestries. Three or four years are often required to make a new one.

A concluding word should be said about the unsung army of workers who protect the art works of the Vatican against the ravages of time. The Holy See maintains a workshop for the care and restoration of these works. Those who perform this task are not known to the public and get little credit for the great service they do, but they have saved for future generations many art treasures which would otherwise have been lost.

INDEX

INDEX

Pontifical University, 24

Pope, army of, 117; assistant to, 54; Coronation of, 19; election of, 12; kingdom of, 79

Pope of the Workingman, 89

Popes: Adrian I, 81; Adrian IV, 84; Alexander VII, 77; Benedict XI, 73; Benedict XV, 90; Clement V, 73; Gregory X, 12, 43; Gregory XI, 73; Julius II, 76; Leo the Great, 80; Leo III, 81; Leo IV, 73; Leo XIII, 89; Nicholas II, 43; Nicholas III, 73; Nicholas V, 75; Pius IX, 85, 89; Pius X, 90; Pius XI, 77, 90, 142; Pius XII, 5, 67, 104, 110; Sergius II, 80; Sixtus IV, 75, 134; Sixtus V, 73; Stephen II, 80; Sylvester, 71; Urban V, 73

President Roosevelt, 31

President Wilson, 27

Princes of the Church, 40

"Prisoner" released, 89

Private and public audiences, 38

Propaganda of the Faith, Congregation of, 50

Radio, papal, 1

Rainbow in the sky, 14

Randall, Alexander W., 63

Raphael, 76

Ratti, Monsignor, 55

Ravenna, 79

Religious, Congregation of, 50

Resignation of Mussolini, 35

Robes of a cardinal, 44

Roman Congregations, 46, 48

Roman Curia, 48

Roman Empire, 79

Roman Question, The, 88; settling of, 93

Roman Tribunals, 46, 48

Rome, bombing of, 35, 106; march on, 96; Sack of, 84

Rossi, Count, 63

Rules of the conclave, 10

Russian Communism, 105

Sack of Rome, 84

Sacrament of Penance, 138

Sacred Penitentiaria, 52

Sacred Rites, Congregation of the, 51

Sacred Roman Rota, 53

Sacristy of St. Peter's, 140

St. Anacletus, 71

St. Catherine of Siena, 73

St. John Lateran, Church of, 93

St. Linus, 70

St. Peter, 69; bronze statue of, 135; Chair of, 136; crucifixion of, 71; death of, 70; tomb of, 2, 128

St. Peter's, 122; Basilica of, 72, 128; Confession of, 131; crypts of, 2; lighting of, 144; Sacristy of, 140

St. Peter's Chair, Feast of, 137

St. Philip Neri, 24

Sala dei Paramenti, 151

Sala del Pappagallo, 151

Sala Ducale, 151

Sanpietrini, 126

Santa Maria, Church of, 24

Saracens, 72

Sarcophagus of Junius Bassus, 141

Sardia, Archbishop of, 26

Sartori, John B., 61

Scala Pia, 148

Scala Regia or Royal Stairs, 148

Secret Archives, 156

Secret consistory, 44

Secretariate of Briefs to Princes, 59

Secretariate of State, 54

Secretary of Latin Letters, 59

Secretary of State, 29

Sedia Gestatoria, 21

Seminaries, Universities, and Studies, Congregation of, 52

Septuagint Bible, 155

Serafini, Marquis Camillo, 110

Sergius II, Pope, 80

Seven Years' War, 61

Sistine Chapel, 75, 151

Sixtus IV, Pope, 75

Sixtus V, Pope, 73

Sladen, Douglas, 56

South America, 29

Spellman, Monsignor Francis J., 101

Station HVJ, 110

States of the Church, 85

Stephen II, Pope, 80

Don Sharkey began his writing career while still in high school by working on a local magazine in Middletown, Ohio, his birthplace. After working as a feature writer for the *Middletown Journal,* he joined the staff of a young people's publication, climbing the ladder from feature and news writer to associate editor, managing editor, and finally editor. Shortly after announcement of his forthcoming book, WHITE SMOKE OVER THE VATICAN, he was besieged by editors demanding articles on this unique country, which he commenced to turn out furiously. Besides numerous magazine articles, he is the author of a juvenile work of fiction, *The Lost Prince,* and a book length magazine serial.